DK Pocket Genius

ROCKS AND MINERALS

FACTS AT YOUR FINGERTIPS

LONDON, NEW YORK, MUNICH,
MELBOURNE, and DELHI

DK DELHI
Project editor Bharti Bedi
Project art editor Deep Shikha Walia
Senior editor Kingshuk Ghoshal
Senior art editor Govind Mittal
Assistant art editor Aanchal Singal
DTP designers Rajesh Singh Adhikari,
Jaypal Singh Chauhan
Picture researcher Sumedha Chopra
Managing editor Saloni Talwar
Managing art editor Romi Chakraborty
CTS manager Balwant Singh
Production manager Pankaj Sharma

DK LONDON
Senior editor Fleur Star
Senior art editor Philip Letsu
US editor Margaret Parrish
Jacket editor Manisha Majithia
Jacket designer Laura Brim
Jacket design development manager
Sophia Tampakopolous
Production editor Ben Marcus
Production controller Mary Slater

Publisher Andrew Macintyre
Associate publishing director Liz Wheeler
Art director Phil Ormerod
Publishing director Jonathan Metcalf

Consultant Kevin Walsh

First published in the United States in 2012
by DK Publishing
375 Hudson Street, New York, New York 10014

Copyright © 2012 Dorling Kindersley Limited
12 13 14 15 16 10 9 8 7 6 5 4 3 2 1
001–184264–Jun/12

A catalog record for this book
is available from the Library of Congress.

ISBN: 978-0-7566-9285-8

Printed and bound by South China
Printing Company, China

**Discover more at
www.dk.com**

CONTENTS

4 Our rocky planet
6 What is a mineral?
8 What is a rock?
10 Be a collector

14 ROCKS

16 How rocks are made
18 Identifying rocks
20 Igneous rocks
30 Sedimentary rocks
42 Metamorphic rocks
52 Meteorites

54 MINERALS

56 Where minerals form
58 Mineral groups
62 Identifying minerals
66 Gemstones
68 Native elements
76 Sulfides
90 Sulfosalts
92 Oxides
98 Hydroxides
100 Halides
104 Carbonates
110 Phosphates, arsenates, and vanadates
116 Nitrates and borates
118 Sulfates, chromates, molybdates, tungstates
122 Silicates
140 Organic gems

144 The periodic table
146 Rock facts
148 Mineral facts
150 Glossary
152 Index
156 Acknowledgments

Scales and sizes
This book contains profiles of rocks and minerals with scale drawings to indicate their size.

6 in
(15 cm)

Our rocky planet

Our planet is like an onion, made up of a number of layers. In the center is a solid core, which is surrounded by the mantle and the crust. We live on the Earth's surface on top of the crust, the thin outer layer that carries oceans and continents. These layers developed early in the Earth's history. During the Earth's formation, denser materials, such as iron, sank to the center, while lighter materials, such as silicates and other minerals, rose to the surface.

Upper mantle is made of warm, mobile rocks

Core and mantle

The core is made up of a solid inner part and a liquid outer part. The mantle is a layer of dense minerals, just above the core. High pressure makes the lower mantle solid, while the minerals in the upper mantle are like a gluey liquid. Molten rocks found inside the Earth are called magma.

Lower mantle contains dense rock formed under pressure

Outer core creates Earth's magnetic field as the molten material moves

Inner core is solid and contains a mixture of iron and nickel

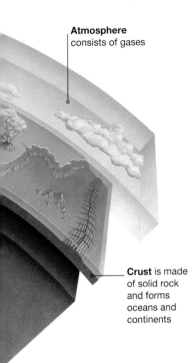

Atmosphere consists of gases

Crust is made of solid rock and forms oceans and continents

The oldest type of rock is Acasta gneiss, which first formed 4.2 billion years ago.

Lava flowing today from Kilauea volcano, Hawaiian Islands, will cool to form igneous rocks.

How old are rocks?

Rocks formed when the Earth was cool enough for them to become solid. The first rock on the Earth solidified around 4.2 billion years ago. Rocks and minerals have been forming ever since and are still forming today—at the Earth's surface, in the crust, on the ocean floor, and in the mantle deep below.

Earth's crust

The crust is made up of "panels" called tectonic plates. When two plates collide, they push against one another, sometimes forming mountains. This tectonic movement may bring up rocks from deep inside the mantle to the surface.

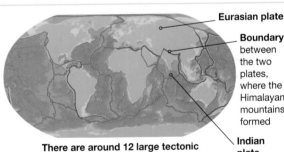

Eurasian plate

Boundary between the two plates, where the Himalayan mountains formed

Indian plate

There are around 12 large tectonic plates on the Earth's crust, both on land and below the seas and oceans.

What is a mineral?

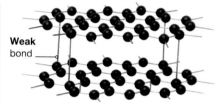

A mineral is a naturally occurring, solid inorganic substance, which means it doesn't come from the remains of plants or animals. It is made from chemical elements—simple substances that cannot be broken down further. Minerals grow or cement together to form rocks.

Green chrysocolla is a mineral

What is a mineral made of?

Minerals are chemical compounds made up of two or more chemical elements. The atoms in the elements bind together to form solid pieces called crystals. Some crystals can grow to several yards wide, but others are so tiny they can only be seen with a microscope.

When crystals have enough room to grow, they form **well-defined shapes**, such as seen in this amethyst.

Weak bond

Graphite structure

Carbon atoms

Strong bond

Diamond structure

Pattern of atoms

The atoms of elements in a mineral form a set pattern that never changes. This pattern gives the mineral its properties, such as hardness, color, and shape. For example, graphite and diamond are both forms of carbon. In graphite, the atoms are linked with weak bonds, which makes it soft. Diamond has strong bonds, making it the hardest mineral.

Feldspar in granite

Rock-forming minerals

Mineralogists (people who study minerals) sometimes group minerals into two types: ore minerals and rock-forming minerals. This group includes feldspar, which is one of the most abundant of all minerals and is found in many types of rock.

Ore minerals

Some minerals are mined for their metal content. Known as ore minerals, they are crushed and separated and then refined and melted to produce metal. This LKAB mine in Sweden is the largest in the world. Most of its ore is magnetite, which is used to produce iron.

MINERAL OR NOT?

Oil rig, North Sea

Although some substances such as **oil** may be called minerals, they come from the remains of living things and are actually classified as hydrocarbons.

Minerals such as rubies, diamonds, and emeralds can be copied and produced in laboratories. Such artificial versions are not true minerals because they do not grow naturally.

Artificial rubies

What is a rock?

A rock is a solid collection of mineral grains that grow or become cemented together. Geologists (people who study rocks and minerals) classify rocks into three main types on the basis of how they are formed—igneous, sedimentary, and metamorphic.

Composition

Every rock is made up of one or more minerals. For example, gabbro, an igneous rock, is made up of minerals including olivine, pyroxene, and plagioclase feldspar.

Plagioclase feldspar
The light grains are a type of feldspar called plagioclase. There are different kinds of feldspar minerals, which form part of most types of rock.

Gabbro

Olivine
This mineral forms only in igneous rocks that solidify below the ground. It contains iron and magnesium.

Thin slice of gabbro seen under a microscope

Pyroxene
This mineral is abundant in the Earth's mantle. Some rocks on the Moon are also made of pyroxene.

TYPES OF ROCK

Igneous rocks form from molten magma that has cooled and hardened on or below the Earth's surface.

Obsidian is an igneous rock

Red color due to iron oxide

Sedimentary rocks form at the Earth's surface and consist of layers of rock fragments, minerals, or organic matter such as sea shells that have been deposited on top of each other.

Red sandstone is a sedimentary rock

Metamorphic rocks can form when rocks are squeezed by pressure and heated deep under the Earth's crust.

Banded gneiss is a metamorphic rock

Be a collector

Rocks and minerals can be found everywhere—up in the mountains, along streams, on beaches, and even on a driveway! Collecting them and recording the finds is a popular hobby that dates back to the 19th century.

Safety first

Protective clothing and shoes may need to be worn at certain collection sites. Rocks can splinter while chipping or trimming, so it is best to wear protective goggles and gloves. A compass and a map are useful for directions.

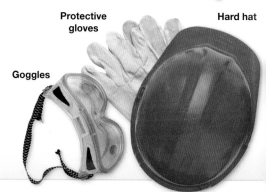

Map and compass

In the field

Before going out in the field to collect rocks, it is a good idea to find out about the site and the kind of specimens expected to be found there. Joining a group of collectors can be more fun and is safer than taking the trip alone.

Protective gloves

Hard hat

Goggles

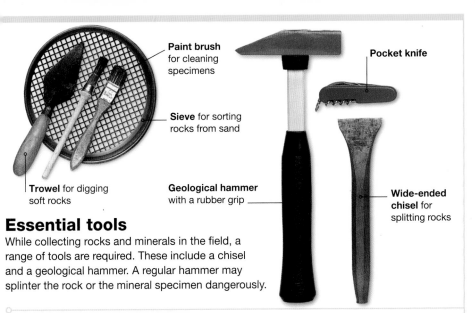

Paint brush for cleaning specimens

Pocket knife

Sieve for sorting rocks from sand

Trowel for digging soft rocks

Geological hammer with a rubber grip

Wide-ended chisel for splitting rocks

Essential tools

While collecting rocks and minerals in the field, a range of tools are required. These include a chisel and a geological hammer. A regular hammer may splinter the rock or the mineral specimen dangerously.

Keeping records

In some cases, it is better to observe and record samples with a camera or in a sketchpad than to remove them from a site, which may damage the rocks. The exact location and details of a find can be recorded in a notebook.

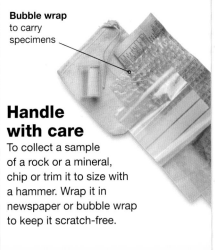

Bubble wrap to carry specimens

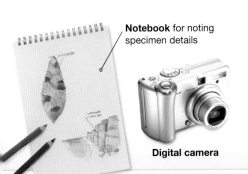

Notebook for noting specimen details

Digital camera

Handle with care

To collect a sample of a rock or a mineral, chip or trim it to size with a hammer. Wrap it in newspaper or bubble wrap to keep it scratch-free.

Cleaning specimens

Most specimens are dirty when collected. Surplus rock fragments can be removed from a specimen by washing them in water. Scrub gently with a brush to remove loose soil and debris when the specimen is dry. Every specimen must be cleaned only as much as needed. It is best to begin with the most gentle method.

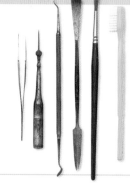

Cleaning tools include tweezers, toothbrushes, and even dental picks

Index cards to list specimens alphabetically and store field notes or other details

Labeling

After the specimens have been identified, label them for future reference, along with notes on their location or other specific details.

Magnifying glass to study and identify rock

Cotton to clean specimens

Plastic box
for brittle pieces

Storage and display

To avoid damage, specimens can be stored in individual trays or boxes. It is useful to keep an index for larger collections, using index cards to record details of the specimens, such as their locations and the dates of collection.

Templates to make cardboard boxes for storage

Rocks

When minerals grow or cement together, they can form rocks. Some rocks, such as dolomite, are made up of only one mineral. However, most rocks are a combination of two or more minerals. Some also contain fossils of plants and animals. New rocks form in different ways—when magma becomes solid, when old rocks break down, or when there is a change in temperature or pressure.

MOAI
Found on Easter Island, the Moai are human figures carved out of pieces of rock called tuff.

How rocks are made

Rocks are formed and destroyed all the time. There are three main ways rocks form. Igneous rocks form when magma and lava solidify. Sedimentary rocks form in layers made up of pieces of existing rock that have been broken down by erosion and weathering. Metamorphic rocks form by heat or pressure.

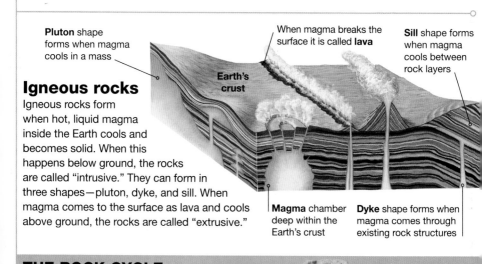

Pluton shape forms when magma cools in a mass

When magma breaks the surface it is called **lava**

Sill shape forms when magma cools between rock layers

Earth's crust

Igneous rocks

Igneous rocks form when hot, liquid magma inside the Earth cools and becomes solid. When this happens below ground, the rocks are called "intrusive." They can form in three shapes—pluton, dyke, and sill. When magma comes to the surface as lava and cools above ground, the rocks are called "extrusive."

Magma chamber deep within the Earth's crust

Dyke shape forms when magma comes through existing rock structures

THE ROCK CYCLE

Rocks are either igneous, sedimentary, or metamorphic. Over thousands of years, rocks can change from one type to another, from igneous to sedimentary to metamorphic and back to igneous. This process is called the rock cycle.

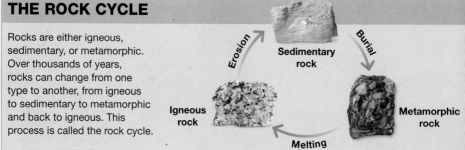

Erosion

Sedimentary rock

Burial

Igneous rock

Melting

Metamorphic rock

Sedimentary rocks

Sedimentary rocks form on, or very near, the Earth's surface where eroded rock particles transported by wind, water, and ice are deposited on dry land, on the beds of rivers and lakes, and in the seas.

Weathering produces sediments that are carried by rivers

Sediments may deposit on the seabed

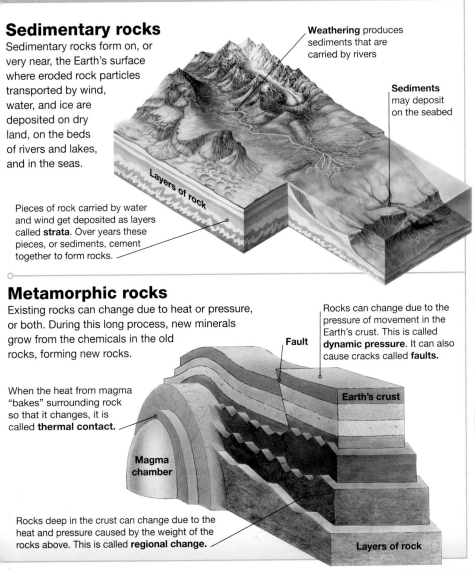

Pieces of rock carried by water and wind get deposited as layers called **strata**. Over years these pieces, or sediments, cement together to form rocks.

Layers of rock

Metamorphic rocks

Existing rocks can change due to heat or pressure, or both. During this long process, new minerals grow from the chemicals in the old rocks, forming new rocks.

Rocks can change due to the pressure of movement in the Earth's crust. This is called **dynamic pressure**. It can also cause cracks called **faults.**

Fault

When the heat from magma "bakes" surrounding rock so that it changes, it is called **thermal contact.**

Earth's crust

Magma chamber

Rocks deep in the crust can change due to the heat and pressure caused by the weight of the rocks above. This is called **regional change.**

Layers of rock

Identifying rocks

Geologists can identify rocks through characteristics such as the size, shape, and arrangement of their grains. Grains in igneous rocks are usually randomly arranged. Sedimentary rocks are made of rock particles and minerals that are cemented together. In metamorphic rocks, the grains are often aligned into patterns, known as foliations.

IGNEOUS ROCK CHARACTERISTICS

Peridotite

Basalt

Pink granite

Large grains

Igneous rocks form below ground when magma in the Earth's crust solidifies. The grains are well-developed and large, since they have enough time to grow. Peridotite is an igneous rock with well-developed grains.

Small grains

When magma erupts from volcanoes and reaches the Earth's surface, it is called lava. When this lava solidifies above the ground, it cools down rapidly. This gives little time for grains to develop. Basalt is an example of an igneous rock with small grains.

Color

The mineral content of an igneous rock can be determined from its color. A light-colored igneous rock, such as pink granite, is rich in silica. Dark-colored rocks have less silica but contain other dark, heavy minerals.

SEDIMENTARY ROCK CHARACTERISTICS

Grain size

The grains in sedimentary rocks are of different sizes and textures. Conglomerate grains are coarse.

Conglomerate

Grain shape

The shape of particles in sedimentary rocks show how the particles were transported. The particles of this sandstone were rounded by desert winds.

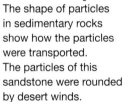

Millet-seed sandstone

Presence of fossils

The presence of fossils is an indicator of rock type. They are very common in sedimentary rocks such as limestone, but rare in metamorphic rocks. Fossils never occur in igneous rocks.

Freshwater limestone

METAMORPHIC ROCK CHARACTERISTICS

Fine grain size

Marble

Size of grains

Grains in metamorphic rocks grow slowly. Large grains indicate that the rock was formed under high pressure and heat. Rocks that form under lower pressure and heat have smaller grains.

Crinkled layers

Folded schist

Foliation

When a metamorphic rock forms under pressure, its grains may line up in patterns. This gives the rock a distinct wavy appearance.

Igneous rocks

The Latin word *ignis* means "fire." Igneous rocks form when hot, molten magma inside the Earth is pushed toward the crust and cools above or below the surface, forming solid rocks.

FOCUS ON...
FORMATIONS
Igneous rocks form some amazing natural structures, and man-made ones, too.

Obsidian

Obsidian forms when lava cools so rapidly that mineral crystals do not have time to grow. In ancient times, Native Americans, Aztecs, and Greeks used obsidian to make weapons, tools, and ornaments.

WHERE FORMED	Above ground
SHAPE WHEN FORMED	Lava flow
GRAIN SIZE	Fine
COLOR	Black, brown
MINERAL CONTENT	Glass

Basalt

When the lava cools and solidifies into basalt on the Earth's surface, it may split into many-sided columns. Basalt forms ocean floors and large outcrops on land, such as the Deccan Traps in India. It is rich in iron and magnesium.

WHERE FORMED	Above ground
SHAPE WHEN FORMED	Lava flow
GRAIN SIZE	Fine to coarse
COLOR	Dark gray to black
MINERAL CONTENT	Pyroxene, plagioclase, olivine, magnetite

▲ The Giant's Causeway, in Northern Ireland, is 40,000 basalt pillars packed closely together.

▲ The Devil's Tower, made of phonolite, was declared a national monument of the United States in 1906.

▲ Sierra Nevada is a huge mass of granite, formed at great depth, brought to the surface.

▲ Mount Rushmore's granite has been carved to show the faces of American presidents.

Granite

Granite is formed deep inside the Earth's crust. It forms when magma cools down slowly. Crushed granite is used as gravel and road-building material. Polished granite is used for kitchen countertops and gravestones.

WHERE FORMED	Below ground
SHAPE WHEN FORMED	Pluton
GRAIN SIZE	Medium to coarse
COLOR	White, light gray, gray, pink, red
MINERAL CONTENT	Feldspars, quartz, mica, hornblende

Dolerite

Dolerite is an extremely hard rock and occurs in fissures in other rocks. You can see the crystals in dolerite with the naked eye.

WHERE FORMED	Below ground
SHAPE WHEN FORMED	Dykes, sills
GRAIN SIZE	Fine to medium
COLOR	Dark gray to black, often mottled white
MINERAL CONTENT	Plagioclase, pyroxene, quartz, magnetite, olivine

Diorite

A prized rock in ancient Egypt, diorite was used to build columns, figures, and sarcophagi (stone coffins), and for lining the chambers of some pyramids.

WHERE FORMED	Below ground
SHAPE WHEN FORMED	Pluton, dyke, sill
GRAIN SIZE	Medium to coarse
COLOR	Mottled black, dark green, gray, white
MINERAL CONTENT	Plagioclase, hornblende, biotite

Rhyolite

Kimberlite

Kimberlite is the major source of diamonds. Kimberley in South Africa was one of the first sites to be mined for diamonds and inspired the name of the rock. However, not every occurrence yields gem-quality diamonds.

WHERE FORMED	Below ground
SHAPE WHEN FORMED	Dyke, pipe
GRAIN SIZE	Fine to coarse
COLOR	Dark gray
MINERAL CONTENT	Olivine, pyroxene, mica, garnet, ilmenite, diamond

Rhyolite is a rare rock that forms from volcanic eruptions. Its lava is very rich in silica, so it is very sticky and may plug the volcano's vent.

WHERE FORMED Above ground

SHAPE WHEN FORMED Lava flow

GRAIN SIZE Fine to coarse

COLOR Very light to medium gray, light pink

MINERAL CONTENT Quartz, potassium feldspar, glass, biotite, amphibole, plagioclase

Andesite

This rock is named after the Andes Mountains of South America. It erupts from volcanoes and is found in areas where one tectonic plate slides under another, such as in the Andes.

WHERE FORMED Above ground

SHAPE WHEN FORMED Lava flow

GRAIN SIZE Fine, with some small grains

COLOR Light to dark gray, reddish-pink

MINERAL CONTENT Feldspars, pyroxene, amphibole, biotite

Peridotite

This rock forms much of the Earth's mantle. Eruptions of magma from the mantle can bring up nodules (lumps) of peridotite to the surface. It is a major source of chromium.

Green olivine

WHERE FORMED Below ground

SHAPE WHEN FORMED Pluton, dyke, sill

GRAIN SIZE Coarse

COLOR Dark green to black

MINERAL CONTENT Olivine, pyroxene, garnet, chromite

Pumice

Highly porous and frothlike, pumice forms when gas-filled liquid magma erupts like a carbonated drink from a shaken bottle and cools quickly. The resulting foam solidifies into a rock that is so light it floats on water.

WHERE FORMED Above ground

SHAPE WHEN FORMED Lava flow

GRAIN SIZE Fine

COLOR White, yellow, gray, black

MINERAL CONTENT Glass, feldspar, quartz

Ignimbrite

This is a type of tuff that is deposited by flowing rivers of ash. Such flows can cause deaths during volcanic eruptions. In June 1912, Novarupta, a volcano in Alaska, produced the largest quantity of ignimbrite in history.

WHERE FORMED Above ground

SHAPE WHEN FORMED Lava flow

GRAIN SIZE Fine

COLOR Pale cream, red-brown, gray

MINERAL CONTENT Igneous rock and crystal fragments, welded volcanic glass

Pélé's hair

Named after the Hawaiian goddess of fire, this rock has a fine, wispy texture. It forms when very liquid magma is spewed out from a volcano and cools rapidly in midair.

WHERE FORMED Above ground

SHAPE WHEN FORMED Lava spray

GRAIN SIZE Very fine

COLOR Pale brown

MINERAL CONTENT Basaltic glass

Tuff

Tuff forms when foaming magma comes up to the surface as a mixture of hot gases and glowing particles and is thrown out from a volcano.

WHERE FORMED Above ground

SHAPE WHEN FORMED
Lava flow

GRAIN SIZE Fine

COLOR Gray, brown, green

MINERAL CONTENT Glassy, crystalline fragments

Syenite

Syenite is an attractive, multicolored rock, which may be polished and used as a decorative stone. It forms large crystals as it cools slowly underground. It looks similar to granite but, unlike granite, it contains little, if any, quartz.

WHERE FORMED Below ground

SHAPE WHEN FORMED Pluton, dyke, sill

GRAIN SIZE Medium to coarse

COLOR Gray, pink, red

MINERAL CONTENT Potassium feldspar, plagioclase, biotite, amphibole, pyroxene, feldspathoids

Dacite

Dacite derives its name from Dacia, a territory in the Roman Empire, where it was first described. It forms part of several volcanoes, such as the one at Crater Lake, Oregon.

WHERE FORMED Above ground

SHAPE WHEN FORMED Pluton, dyke, sill

GRAIN SIZE Fine

COLOR Gray to black

MINERAL CONTENT Plagioclase, quartz, pyroxene, amphibole, biotite

Anorthosite

The ancient, light-colored highlands on the far side of the Moon are made of anorthosite. It forms large masses or layers between rocks such as gabbro and peridotite.

WHERE FORMED Below ground

SHAPE WHEN FORMED Lava flow

GRAIN SIZE Medium to coarse

COLOR Light gray to white

MINERAL CONTENT Plagioclase, olivine, pyroxene, magnetite

Trachyte

The name "trachyte" comes from the Greek word for "rough." This tough and resistant rock has been used for paving roads for thousands of years.

WHERE FORMED Above ground

SHAPE WHEN FORMED Lava flow, dyke, sill

GRAIN SIZE Fine to medium

COLOR Off-white, gray, pale yellow, pink

MINERAL CONTENT
Sanidine, plagioclase, feldspathoids, quartz, olivine, pyroxene, biotite

Rhomb porphyry

Porphyry refers to igneous rocks with large-grained crystals. Rhomb porphyry gets its name from the rhombic, or diamond, shape of its large crystals.

WHERE FORMED Above ground

SHAPE WHEN FORMED Lava flow, dyke, sill

GRAIN SIZE Medium

COLOR Gray-white, red-brown, purple

MINERAL CONTENT Feldspar

Pegmatite

Pegmatite is one of the sources of important ore minerals, which provide useful metals such as tungsten. Pegmatites are also important sources of some gemstones, and mica.

WHERE FORMED Below ground

SHAPE WHEN FORMED Pluton

GRAIN SIZE Very coarse

COLOR Pink, white, cream

MINERAL CONTENT Quartz, feldspar, mica, tourmaline, topaz

The Devil's Tower is **sacred** to many Native-American Plains tribes, who call it "Bear's Tipi"

DEVIL'S TOWER

The Devil's Tower in Wyoming is a giant structure of phonolite, an igneous rock. It formed when a volcano erupted and the magma cooled and solidified to form underground columns. Over millions of years, its surrounding layers weathered away, leaving the columns exposed.

FOCUS ON...
USE IN ART
The colors from some sedimentary rocks have been used by artists for a long time.

▲ Chalk was used to make the first white coloring for art.

▲ Clay was often used by early artists for extracting the color brown.

Sedimentary rocks

Sedimentary rocks make up 80–90 percent of the rocks on the Earth's surface. These rocks form on land when sediments or grains join together. They may be carried by wind or water to the sea where they are buried and form layers of rock.

Limestone

Fine texture

Fossil of shell

Limestone forms in warm, shallow seas and is made of the mineral calcite, which comes from seawater or the shells and skeletons of sea animals. It is used as a building stone and as a raw material in manufacturing glass. On burning it produces lime, which is used to make cement.

ORIGIN Seabed

GRAIN SIZE Fine to medium, angular to rounded

COLOR White, gray, pink

MINERAL CONTENT Calcite

FOSSILS Marine and freshwater invertebrates, plants

Rock gypsum

Also known as gyprock, rock gypsum forms when water evaporates from oceans or salty lakes. It is used as a fertilizer and to make drywall.

ORIGIN Seabed

GRAIN SIZE Medium to fine crystalline

COLOR White, pinkish, yellowish, gray

MINERAL CONTENT Gypsum

FOSSILS None

Dolomite

Dolomite rock is formed entirely of the mineral dolomite. The Swiss Alps in Italy, also known as the Dolomites, are almost entirely composed of this rock.

Compact carbonate rock

ORIGIN Land

GRAIN SIZE Fine to medium, crystalline

COLOR Gray to yellowish-gray

MINERAL CONTENT Dolomite

FOSSILS Invertebrates

Rock salt

Rock salt forms when salty water evaporates. In addition to being used in kitchens as table salt, it is used to make soaps and baking soda, among other things.

ORIGIN Seabed

GRAIN SIZE Coarse to fine crystalline

COLOR White, orange-brown, blue

MINERAL CONTENT Halite

FOSSILS None

Chalk

Chalk is made up of the mineral calcite, which comes from the shells and skeletons of sea animals. The grains in chalk are so small that they cannot be seen without a magnifying glass.

ORIGIN Seabed

GRAIN SIZE Very fine, angular to rounded

COLOR White, gray, buff

MINERAL CONTENT Calcite

FOSSILS Invertebrates, vertebrates

Peat

As plants decay over thousands of years, they slowly turn into coal. The formation of peat is the first step in this process. Peat forms in warm, moist climates, where there are enough nutrients, bacteria, and oxygen.

ORIGIN Land

GRAIN SIZE Medium, fine

COLOR Dark brown to black

MINERAL CONTENT Carbon

FOSSILS Plants, invertebrates

Anthracite

This form of coal contains a lot of carbon. It is glassy and cleaner to handle than other forms. Anthracite burns at a high temperature, with a blue flame, and produces very little smoke. It can be polished to make decorative items.

ORIGIN Land

GRAIN SIZE Fine

COLOR Shiny black

MINERAL CONTENT
Carbon

FOSSILS Plants

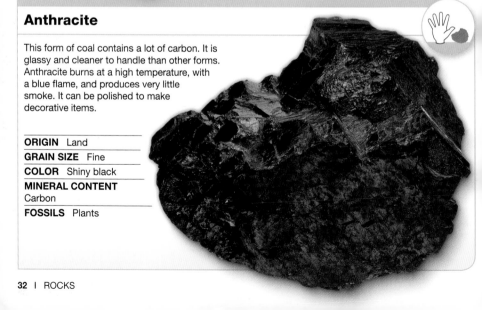

Travertine

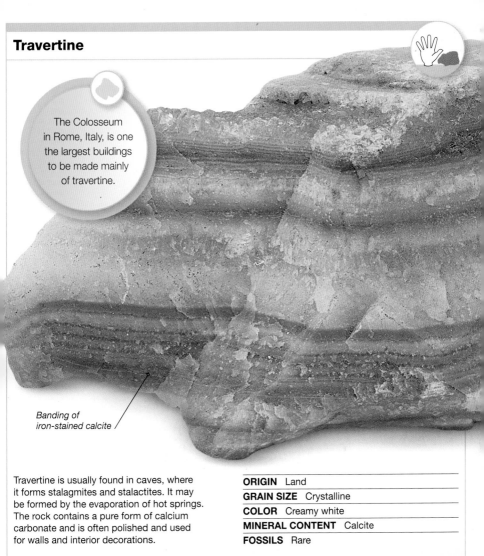

The Colosseum in Rome, Italy, is one the largest buildings to be made mainly of travertine.

Banding of iron-stained calcite

Travertine is usually found in caves, where it forms stalagmites and stalactites. It may be formed by the evaporation of hot springs. The rock contains a pure form of calcium carbonate and is often polished and used for walls and interior decorations.

ORIGIN	Land
GRAIN SIZE	Crystalline
COLOR	Creamy white
MINERAL CONTENT	Calcite
FOSSILS	Rare

Chert

This rock is so hard, it can't be scratched with a knife. In the Stone Age, it was used for making tools and weapons. Today, chert is used in building roads and can even be polished to make jewelry.

ORIGIN	Seabed, or as nodules in limestone
GRAIN SIZE	Fine, crystalline
COLOR	Grayish
MINERAL CONTENT	Chalcedony
FOSSILS	Invertebrates, plants

Loess

The German word *loess* means "loose" and refers to the loose deposits of this rock by glacial winds. Loess is soft and crumbly and contains few clay minerals, so it feels smooth, not sticky, when wet.

ORIGIN	Land
GRAIN SIZE	Very fine
COLOR	Yellowish or brownish
MINERAL CONTENT	Quartz, feldspar
FOSSILS	Rare

Tufa

Tufa is formed when lime-rich water evaporates, leaving behind calcium carbonate. It gets deposited on cliffs, caves, and rock surfaces in regions where rainfall is low. In the process of formation, some pebbles and grains of sediments also get caught in it.

Flint

In prehistoric times, people used flakes of flint to make sharp-edged weapons including knives, scrapers, and arrowheads. Flint is a hard substance, rich in silica, and it is found as bands in limestone.

ORIGIN Nodules in limestone or dolomite
GRAIN SIZE Fine, crystalline
COLOR Gray
MINERAL CONTENT Chalcedony
FOSSILS Invertebrates

Tufa towers form under water and can reach heights of more than 30 ft (9 m).

ORIGIN Land
GRAIN SIZE Fine, crystalline
COLOR White or orange-stained
MINERAL CONTENT Calcite or silica
FOSSILS Rare

Feldspathic gritstone

This rock is made up of sand-sized grains and gravel. Iron oxides may help bind the grains together.

Feldspar grain

ORIGIN Seabed, land
GRAIN SIZE Coarse to medium, angular
COLOR Brownish with a tinge of pink
MINERAL CONTENT Quartz, feldspar, mica
FOSSILS Invertebrates, vertebrates, plants

Shale

Shale is a highly fissile rock, meaning it breaks up into thin sheets. It forms from fine muds in various environments. Some shales have important deposits of oil in them.

ORIGIN Seabed, freshwater, glacier

GRAIN SIZE Fine

COLOR Gray

MINERAL CONTENT
Clays, quartz, calcite

FOSSILS Invertebrates, vertebrates, plants

Breccia

Sandstone

Gaps between grains form different textures

Sandstones are classified by their different textures, which form from the way the sand-sized grains are cemented together. It is used as a building stone since it is durable.

ORIGIN Land

GRAIN SIZE Fine to medium, angular to rounded

COLOR Cream to red

MINERAL CONTENT
Quartz, feldspar

FOSSILS Vertebrates, invertebrates, plants

Breccia is a rock made up of generally large, rough grains cemented together. The lack of rounded grains shows that the rocks have not been transported far.

ORIGIN Seabed, freshwater, glacier

GRAIN SIZE Very coarse, angular

COLOR Varies

MINERAL CONTENT Any hard mineral can be present

FOSSILS Very rare

Conglomerate

Rocks that lie in water for a very long time become smooth and rounded. When these rocks are held together by cement, they form a conglomerate and may get transported long distances. Pebbles are the small rocks; cobbles are medium-sized rocks; and boulders are large. All these are larger than 0.8 in (2 mm) in size.

ORIGIN Seabed, freshwater, glacier

GRAIN SIZE Very coarse, rounded

COLOR Varies

MINERAL CONTENT Any hard mineral can be present

FOSSILS Very rare

Arkose

This granitelike form of sandstone is different from other sandstones since it has more feldspar. It has a rough texture and its grains are usually cemented together by calcite.

ORIGIN Seabed, freshwater

GRAIN SIZE Medium, angular

COLOR Pinkish to pale gray

MINERAL CONTENT Quartz, feldspar

FOSSILS Rare

Ironstone

Sandstones and limestones with more than 15 percent iron content are called ironstones. These ancient rocks formed when there was not as much oxygen in the atmosphere as today.

ORIGIN Seabed or land

GRAIN SIZE Fine to medium, crystalline to angular, oolitic

COLOR Red, black, gray, striped

MINERAL CONTENT Hematite, goethite, chamosite, magnetite, siderite, limonite, jasper

FOSSILS Invertebrates

Clay

Clay grains are so fine that they can't even be seen with a microscope. Damp clay feels sticky, but adding water can make it flexible so it can be molded into different forms and shapes from pots and bricks to ornaments.

ORIGIN Seabed, freshwater, land

GRAIN SIZE Fine

COLOR Dark to light gray, white

MINERAL CONTENT Clay minerals, such as kaolinite, illite, montmorillonite

FOSSILS Plants, invertebrates, vertebrates

Micaceous sandstone

This sandstone contains a high quantity of mica minerals. The mica appears as small flakes in the rock, which are very light and easily blown away in sediments deposited on land. This shows that it's more likely to have been deposited in water.

ORIGIN Seabed or freshwater

GRAIN SIZE Medium, angular to flattened

COLOR Buff, green, gray, pink

MINERAL CONTENT Quartz, feldspar, mica

FOSSILS Invertebrates, plants, vertebrates

Septarian nodule

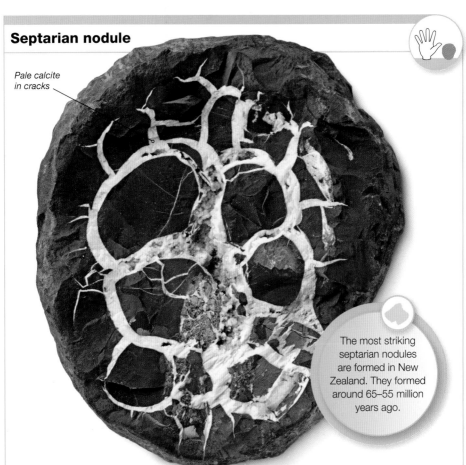

Pale calcite in cracks

The most striking septarian nodules are formed in New Zealand. They formed around 65–55 million years ago.

Nodules and concretions are features that develop after a sedimentary rock forms. Concretions are made of the same minerals as the host rock, but nodules have a different mineral content. Septarian nodules are harder than the surrounding rock. They form when a nodule shrinks and cracks. The cracks fill up with light-colored minerals such as calcite.

ORIGIN Seabed, land

GRAIN SIZE Fine to medium, angular to rounded

COLOR Cream to red

MINERAL CONTENT Calcite or celestine

FOSSILS Vertebrates, invertebrates, plants

The Wave is made of **190** million-year-old sand dunes that have turned to rock

THE WAVE

The Wave, in Arizona, is a natural formation of sandstone rocks that look like a cresting ocean wave. The different layers have been formed by wind deposition. The rocks' varied colors are caused by the presence of different minerals, including hematite.

Metamorphic rocks

When pressure and temperature act upon existing rocks, the atoms and minerals rearrange to form new rocks. These are called metamorphic rocks.

▲ This marble Arch of Constantine in Rome, Italy, was built in the 4th century CE.

▲ The Taj Mahal in Agra, India, is a huge tomb made of marble.

▲ Michelangelo's statue of David was carved from marble between 1501 and 1504.

Phyllite

Wavy foliation

Phyllite is a dark colored rock with an irregular surface. The large grains of mica in it make it shiny. It is sometimes used for making sidewalks.

ORIGINAL ROCK	Mudstone, shale
HOW FORMED	Regional change
TEMPERATURE	Low to moderate
PRESSURE	Low
COLOR	Silvery to greenish-gray

Marble

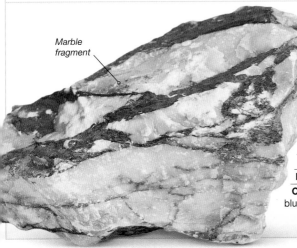

Marble fragment

Pure marble is white. Impurities can make it multicolored. Some marbles, such as pink and green marble, take their common names from their color or mineral impurities.

ORIGINAL ROCK	Limestone
HOW FORMED	Regional change, thermal contact
TEMPERATURE	High
PRESSURE	Low to high
COLOR	White, pink, green, blue, gray

Slate

Slate is an important roofing material and was also used to make chalkboards. It is quarried in large pieces, for use in electrical panels. Plant and animal fossils can be preserved in slate.

ORIGINAL ROCK	Clay, mudstones, shale, tuff
HOW FORMED	Regional change
TEMPERATURE	Low
PRESSURE	Low
COLOR	Gray, purple, green

Schist

Schist rock has visible mineral grains in it. It is rich in micas or chlorite and splits easily along crinkly surfaces.

ORIGINAL ROCK	Mud- and clay-based rocks
HOW FORMED	Regional change
TEMPERATURE	Low to moderate
PRESSURE	Low to moderate
COLOR	Silvery, green

Hornfels

This rock forms at temperatures as high as 1,472°F (800°C). There are many varieties, depending on the minerals in the rock. Hornfels rock is hard to break.

Hornblende and plagioclase

ORIGINAL ROCK	Almost any rock
HOW FORMED	Thermal contact
TEMPERATURE	Moderate to high
PRESSURE	Low to high
COLOR	Dark gray, brown, greenish, reddish

Amphibolite

Roads are often built using amphibolite to give them strength and durability. This rock is also used as an ornamental stone.

ORIGINAL ROCK	Basalt graywacke, dolomite
HOW FORMED	Regional change
TEMPERATURE	Low to moderate
PRESSURE	Low to moderate
COLOR	Gray, black, greenish

Quartzite

Quartzite is formed when sandstones are buried, heated, and squeezed. Quartzite is made up of 90 percent quartz. It is quarried for use as raw material for building roads, laying roofs, and paving blocks.

ORIGINAL ROCK Sandstone
HOW FORMED Regional change
TEMPERATURE High
PRESSURE Low to high
COLOR White, pink

Fulgurite

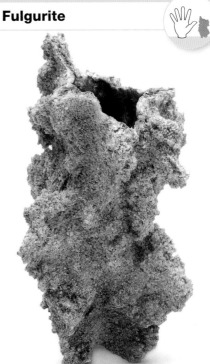

The word fulgurite comes from the Latin *fulgur,* meaning "thunderbolt." This rock forms when lightning strikes sand. Lightning in deserts tends to melt the sand, which then fuses into a fulgurite, forming tubes and crusts.

ORIGINAL ROCK Usually sand
HOW FORMED Thermal contact
TEMPERATURE Very high
PRESSURE Low
COLOR Gray, white, black

Skarn

Skarn is rich in carbonate, calcium, iron, and magnesium silicates. These form different-colored patches in the rock. Some skarn minerals are rich sources of metals and can be valuable deposits of gold, copper, iron, tin, and zinc.

ORIGINAL ROCK
Limestone, dolomite

HOW FORMED
Thermal contact

TEMPERATURE High

PRESSURE Low

COLOR Brown

Typical veined and banded structure

Dark mineral bands

Migmatite

Migmatite means "mixed rock." It consists of gneiss or schists mixed with granite. The granite melts slightly, forming streaks that are lighter in color than the dark bands of gneiss or schists.

ORIGINAL ROCK Various, including granite and gneiss

HOW FORMED
Regional change

TEMPERATURE High

PRESSURE High

COLOR Banded light and dark gray, pink, white

Serpentinite

This rock is the state rock of California. It forms deep within the Earth's crust where tectonic plates meet. Made up of serpentine minerals, this rock is known for its marblelike look and feel.

ORIGINAL ROCK Peridotite

HOW FORMED Regional change

TEMPERATURE Low

PRESSURE High

COLOR Mottled green

Gneiss

This rock is usually found buried deep in mountain-building regions that experience great heat and pressure. Since it does not split easily, gneiss is used as a building material for flooring and facing stones. It is also used as an ornamental stone for countertops and even headstones.

ORIGINAL ROCK	Granite, shale, granodiorite, mudstone, siltstone, or felsic volcanics
HOW FORMED	Regional change
TEMPERATURE	High
PRESSURE	High
COLOR	Gray, pink, multicolored

Mylonite

Mylonite is a crushed rock. It forms on fault planes when movements in the Earth's crust exert great pressure but little heat. The pressure exerted on the rock gives it a wavy texture.

ORIGINAL ROCK	Varies
HOW FORMED	Dynamic pressure
TEMPERATURE	Low
PRESSURE	High
COLOR	Dark or light

Eclogite

Found in the uppermost part of the Earth's mantle, eclogite forms at very high temperatures and pressures. It is a coarse-grained rock that is made up of two main minerals—green omphacite pyroxene and red garnet—and often quartz, too.

ORIGINAL ROCK	Igneous rocks
HOW FORMED	Regional change
TEMPERATURE	High
PRESSURE	High
COLOR	Pale green, red

Gneiss is named either from the old German word for spark or the old Saxon word for **decayed and rotten**

BANDED GNEISS
This gneiss rock has been eroded and polished by
river water rushing past. This reveals the bands
of different minerals that separated and folded
into layers as the rock formed. Gneiss forms
under very high temperature and pressure.

Meteorites

When parts of rocky asteroids and comets break off in space and fall to the Earth, they are called meteorites. Since they come from space, they are not classified as igneous, sedimentary, or metamorphic.

FOCUS ON...
CRATERS

When a meteorite lands on the Earth, it can cause a large impact crater.

Achondrites

Stony meteorites are classified as chondrites and achondrites. The latter are those that do not contain chondrules—miniature igneous rocks that formed in space. Achondrites resemble the rocks found in the Earth's mantle and crust.

ORIGIN	Space
GRAIN SIZE	Medium to coarse
COLOR	Black, gray, yellow
MINERAL CONTENT	Pyroxene, olivine, plagioclase feldspar
FOSSILS	None

Tektite

When large meteorites hit the Earth, they can melt rocks on our planet, which can get thrown in the air and quickly cool to form glass. These glassy objects are called tektites, from the Greek word for "melted."

ORIGIN	Meteorite impact
GRAIN SIZE	Crystalline
COLOR	Green, black
MINERAL CONTENT	Silicate
FOSSILS	None

▲ The 550-ft- (168-m-) deep Barringer Meteorite Crater in Arizona is one of the best known impact craters on the Earth.

▲ The circular Lac à l'Eau Claire, or the Clearwater Lakes, in Quebec, Canada, were formed by meteorite impacts around 210 million years ago.

Stony-iron meteorites

These are mixtures of iron and silicate minerals. Stony-iron meteorites help scientists understand planets such as Mars, which has iron and silicate materials.

ORIGIN Space

GRAIN SIZE Fine to medium

COLOR Gray, greenish, tan, or black

MINERAL CONTENT Olivine, pyroxene, plagioclase

FOSSILS None

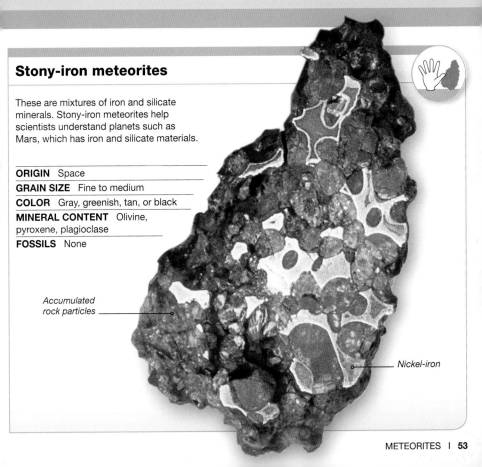

Accumulated rock particles

Nickel-iron

Minerals

Minerals are all around us. There are more than 4,500 known minerals, but only 100 of these are common. They are naturally occurring solids that are made up of particular combinations of chemicals. Minerals make up much of our planet and provide many things we use every day, from copper pipes to jewelry to toothpaste.

MALACHITE BOX
This malachite jewel box was made in 1989. Polished malachite is a popular decorative material for buildings and ornaments.

Where minerals form

Minerals form in many different environments—in rocks, in the sea, inside the Earth, and even in human bones. The way they grow may be affected by temperature and pressure. Some minerals take thousands of years to develop, while others grow in only a few hours.

Sedimentary minerals

Minerals can form on the Earth's surface. When hot, mineral-rich, salty water evaporates, the minerals left behind are known as evaporites. Calcite, which forms limestone rocks, also develops in seawater.

Wulfenite deposits in cracks of lead ore

Mineral veins

Water found in hot springs and beneath volcanoes often carries dissolved minerals. These are deposited in cracks and cavities of rocks, forming mineral veins.

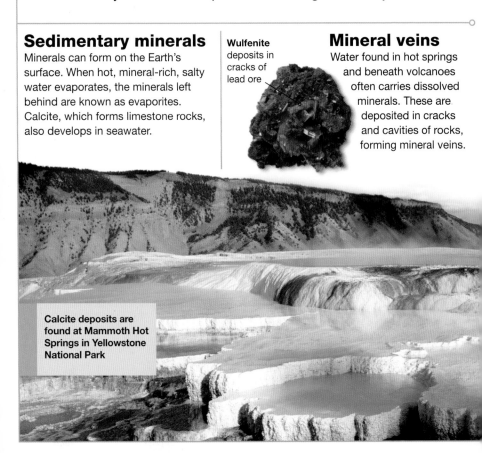

Calcite deposits are found at Mammoth Hot Springs in Yellowstone National Park

Olivine is found in igneous rocks

Metamorphic minerals

In mountain-forming areas, heat and pressure change existing rocks, and new minerals grow. These metamorphic minerals usually have a good crystal shape. Some minerals, such as garnet, form over hundreds of thousands of years as heat and pressure gradually alter the rocks.

Igneous minerals

Magma inside the Earth contains chemicals that are present in minerals. The minerals develop when magma and lava begin to cool and solidify to form igneous rocks.

The mineral spinel grows when metamorphic rocks change

Mineral groups

There are thousands of minerals on the Earth. These have been divided into 12 main groups, or families, based on the chemicals they contain. While some minerals are abundant, others—including diamonds—are very rare and highly prized.

Gold in quartz

Native elements

Most minerals are made from combinations of chemical elements, but a few elements, such as silver, gold, and sulfur, occur naturally by themselves. These are known as native elements.

Sulfides

Sulfur combines with metals to form sulfides. They form near geothermal springs or in veins with quartz. Sulfides include cinnabar and pyrite.

Cinnabar is a mercury sulfide

Sulfosalts

This a group of 200 rare minerals that form when sulfur combines with a metal (silver, copper, lead, or iron) and a semimetal (arsenic or antimony).

Proustite contains arsenic

Oxides

Oxides form when oxygen combines with metals. They include ores (minerals from which metals are extracted) and gems.

Rutile forms when titanium and oxygen combine

Hydroxides

These minerals form when a metallic element combines with hydrogen and oxygen. These minerals are less dense than oxides and tend to be softer. Hydroxides are also important ore minerals. They include bauxite, which is an ore of aluminum.

Bauxite

Halides

In these soft minerals, metals combine with chlorine, bromine, fluorine, or iodine. For example, sylvite is a combination of potassium and chlorine.

Glassy, cube-shaped **crystals**

Sylvite

Carbonates

These form when carbon and oxygen combine with metals. Carbonates are soft and dissolve easily in acidic substances.

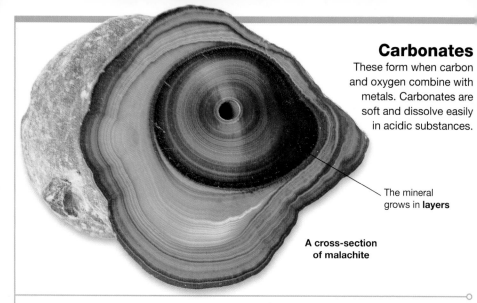

The mineral grows in **layers**

A cross-section of malachite

Erythrite is an arsenate

Phosphates, arsenates, and vanadates

These rare minerals are grouped together because they have a similar structure, made up of oxygen combined with phosphorus, arsenic, or vanadium. They often have vivid colors.

Borates and nitrates

Borates form when a metallic element combines with boron and oxygen. When nitrogen and oxygen combine with a metallic element, nitrates are formed.

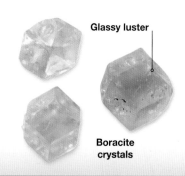

Glassy luster

Boracite crystals

Chalcanthite is a sulfate

Sulfates, chromates, molybdates, tungstates

Around 200 minerals make up this large group. They share a similar structure and elements—oxygen combined with a metal or semimetal. These minerals are dense, brittle, and may be vividly colored.

Silicates

This group makes up a quarter of all known minerals. As well as being common, silicates such as feldspar and quartz are important rock-forming minerals. Other silicates include mica, garnet, and natrolite. All silicates contain silicon and oxygen.

Natrolite

Organic minerals

These are a group of minerals that form from living things, and may or may not have a crystal structure. Amber, coral, and pearl are organic gems. Amber forms from the resin of conifer trees, coral from sea creatures, and pearl comes from certain shellfish and oysters.

Red coral

Identifying minerals

There are many ways to identify a mineral, including observing its color and shape, and how it looks when it reflects light. The hardness of a mineral can be measured by how easily it scratches.

Crystal systems

Minerals have different "crystal systems," or crystal shapes. There are six groups:

| Cubic | Monoclinic | Triclinic | Trigonal/hexagonal | Orthorhombic | Tetragonal |

Cleavage

Cleavage describes how easily and cleanly a mineral breaks along its natural weak points. Perfect cleavage produces a smooth, shiny surface. Cleavage can also be difficult, distinct, or "none" (leaving rough, uneven surfaces).

Obsidian fractures with a conchoidal, or shell-like, pattern

Iceland spar, a type of calcite, cleaves to make a perfect rhombic shape

Fracture

This is how cleanly a mineral breaks in places other than its cleavage lines. Fractures can leave jagged edges (hackly), rough but flat surfaces (even), shell-like scoops (conchoidal), or no pattern at all (uneven).

Habit

A mineral's habit, or general shape, depends on the pattern that its crystals form as they grow. If there is no clear shape, it is called "massive."

Scolecite looks like needles

Copper has a plantlike shape

Actinolite looks like knife blades

Beryl looks like a prism with a regular shape

Fingernail:
2.5

Hardness

Mohs' scale, invented by the mineralogist Friedrich Mohs, measures how hard a mineral is based on how easily it scratches. The scale consists of 10 minerals arranged from 1 to 10. The higher the number, the harder the mineral. Every mineral can scratch the ones listed below it and get scratched by minerals above it on the scale.

MOHS' SCALE OF HARDNESS

| 1: Talc | 2: Gypsum | 3: Calcite | 4: Fluorite | 5: Apatite |
| 6: Orthoclase | 7: Quartz | 8: Topaz | 9: Corundum | 10: Diamond |

Specific gravity (SG)

This is a measure of how heavy a mineral is compared to an equal volume of water.

The SG of jasper is 2.7, meaning it is 2.7 times heavier than water.

Color

Some minerals come in more than one color. Usually this is because the mineral contains impurities or its crystals are flawed.

Fluorite is known for its many different colors.

Streak

If a mineral is crushed up into a powder and drawn on porcelain, it produces a streak. The color of the streak may not be the same as the mineral color.

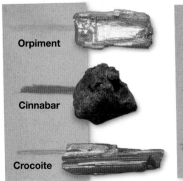

Orpiment

Cinnabar

Crocoite

Chalcopyrite

Hematite

Molybdenite

Transparency

If light can pass through a mineral, it is called translucent. If a mineral is opaque, no light can pass through it. Transparent minerals are clear and see-through.

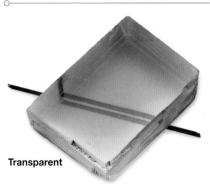

Transparent

Translucent

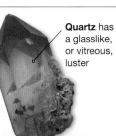

Opaque

Luster

This describes how shiny a mineral is when sunlight reflects off it. Lusters include dull, greasy, silky, metallic, waxy, and vitreous (glassy). The shiniest is adamantine (diamondlike).

Galena looks like metal when light reflects off it

Quartz has a glasslike, or vitreous, luster

Metallic

Vitreous

Gemstones

Some minerals are brilliantly colored and form striking and large crystals that are used as gemstones. They are valued for their beauty and rarity—there's nothing chemical that makes gemstones different from other minerals. More than 4,500 minerals exist, but only 100 are used as gemstones.

Gemstones often look **dull** before they are cut and polished

Uncut Burmese ruby crystal

Cutting and polishing

To bring out the beauty of gemstones, they are cut and polished. Colored stones, such as rubies, are cut in different ways to bring out the rich colors. Opaque or translucent stones are generally cut into a smooth oval. Some gems may be beautiful but too soft or brittle to be cut and worn.

Different cuts bring out the beauty of a gemstone

Mixed cut ruby

Brilliant cut aquamarine

Step cut zircon

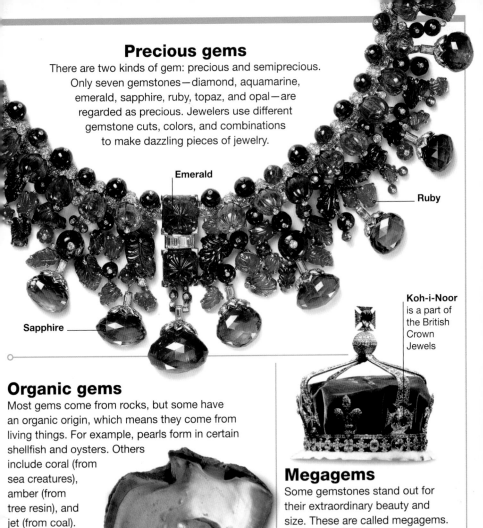

Precious gems

There are two kinds of gem: precious and semiprecious. Only seven gemstones—diamond, aquamarine, emerald, sapphire, ruby, topaz, and opal—are regarded as precious. Jewelers use different gemstone cuts, colors, and combinations to make dazzling pieces of jewelry.

Emerald

Ruby

Koh-i-Noor is a part of the British Crown Jewels

Sapphire

Organic gems

Most gems come from rocks, but some have an organic origin, which means they come from living things. For example, pearls form in certain shellfish and oysters. Others include coral (from sea creatures), amber (from tree resin), and jet (from coal).

Pearl on oyster shell

Megagems

Some gemstones stand out for their extraordinary beauty and size. These are called megagems. The Koh-i-Noor diamond weighs 109 carats (0.77 oz/21.8 g).

FOCUS ON...
GOLD
Aside from being used in jewelry, gold has many other applications.

▲ Worldwide, dentists use about 50 lb (23 kg) of gold a day for making tooth fillings.

▲ Many microchips in computers are made of gold circuits that allow data to flow in the computer.

▲ The plastic visor of an astronaut's spacesuit helmet is coated with gold to protect the astronaut from the Sun's glare.

Native elements

Chemical elements that occur in nature by themselves rather than with other elements are called native elements. They can be classified into three groups: metals, semimetals, and nonmetals.

Copper

Native copper is found close to the Earth's surface above other copper deposits. Copper in its natural state was probably the first metal used by people, who made it into weapons and tools as a substitute for stone. It is now used in electrical wires and deep-sea cables, among other things.

HARDNESS 2.5–3	**SG** 8.9
COLOR Copper-red to brown	
TRANSPARENCY Opaque	
LUSTER Metallic	

Platinum

Platinum is rarer than gold. In addition to being used in jewelry, it is also used to refine fuel to reduce pollution from cars.

HARDNESS 4–4.5	**SG** 14–19
COLOR Whitish steel-gray	
TRANSPARENCY Opaque	
LUSTER Metallic	

Gold

Gold has been a measure of wealth since ancient times. It is ideal for making jewelry because it is soft and can be easily worked into different shapes. Jewelers sometimes mix it with metals such as silver and copper to make it harder. Gold is also valued because it does not lose its color or luster when exposed to air. South Africa is the largest producer of gold in the world.

HARDNESS 2.5–3	**SG** 19.3
COLOR Golden-yellow	
TRANSPARENCY Opaque	
LUSTER Metallic	

Silver

A strong conductor of electricity and heat, silver is widely used in the electrical industry. It is a popular raw material in the making of jewelry and coins. The leading producer of silver is Peru.

HARDNESS 2.5–3	**SG** 10.1–11.1
COLOR Silver-white	
TRANSPARENCY Opaque	
LUSTER Metallic	

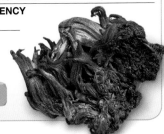

Sulfur

The ancient Chinese discovered how to make gunpowder from sulfur.

Sulfur forms around hot springs and volcanic craters. It burns with a blue flame if held over a lighted match. Mined on a large scale, sulfur is widely used in explosives, fertilizers, dyes, drugs, and detergents.

HARDNESS	1.5–2.5
SG	2.1
COLOR	Yellow
TRANSPARENCY	Transparent to translucent
LUSTER	Resinous to greasy

Diamond

A pure form of carbon, diamond is the hardest mineral on the Earth. Diamond-tipped drills and saws can cut through any substance. The glittery brilliance of diamond makes it the most valuable gemstone in the world.

HARDNESS 10   **SG** 3.4–3.5

COLOR White to black, colorless, yellow, pink, red, blue, brown

TRANSPARENCY Transparent to opaque

LUSTER Diamondlike

Graphite

This mineral takes its name from the Greek word *graphein*, which means "to write." It leaves a black mark when rubbed on paper and is used in pencils. It is also one of the softest minerals and can be cut with a knife.

HARDNESS 1–2

SG 2.2

COLOR Black

TRANSPARENCY Opaque

LUSTER Metallic or dull earthy

Iron

Iron makes up 5 percent of the Earth's crust. After oxygen, silicon, and aluminum, it is the fourth most abundant chemical in the crust. It is used to make a vast number of things, including steel, magnets, and car parts.

HARDNESS 4.5   **SG** 7.3–7.9

COLOR Steel-gray to iron-black

TRANSPARENCY Opaque

LUSTER Metallic

Nickel-iron

Often found in meteorites on the Earth's surface, nickel-iron used to be called "sky-iron" by the ancient Egyptians. They used it to make sacred tools for mummifying pharaohs.

HARDNESS 4-5   **SG** 7.3–8.2

COLOR Steel-gray, dark gray, blackish

TRANSPARENCY Opaque

LUSTER Metallic

Bismuth

This rare native element is mostly found in hydrothermal veins and pegmatites. It is a semimetal—it expands on freezing, just as water expands when it turns into ice.

HARDNESS 2–2.5

SG 9.7–9.8

COLOR Silver-white with reddish tarnish

TRANSPARENCY Opaque

LUSTER Metallic

Arsenic

When heated, this mineral quickly turns into gas without melting. Though poisonous, it was used in some medicines to treat infections. Arsenic was also used to make pesticides.

HARDNESS 3.5

SG 5.7

COLOR Tin-white

TRANSPARENCY Opaque

LUSTER Metallic or dull earthy

Mercury

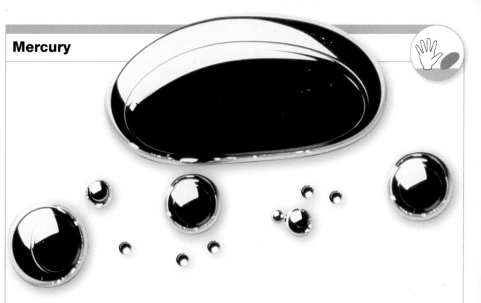

Native mercury exists in a poisonous, liquid form at room temperature. It is used in thermometers because even a minor change in temperature can cause it to expand or contract.

HARDNESS	Liquid		SG	13.6–14.4
COLOR	Silver-white			
TRANSPARENCY	Opaque			
LUSTER	Metallic			

Mercury was named after the Roman god of trade.

The **deepest** point in the
Danakil Desert is 330 ft (100 m) below sea level

SULFUR
The Earth's lowest lying desert, the Danakil in Ethiopia, is known for its extreme heat. It is made up of volcanoes, hot springs, and acidic ponds. Bright yellow sulfur crystallizes around volcanic craters, adding beautiful shapes and color to the landscape.

Sulfides

In these minerals, sulfur combines with one or more metals. They have a metallic luster and can conduct electricity, but not as well as metals. They are important sources of lead, zinc, iron, and copper and a good source of silver and platinum.

Galena

A valuable mineral since Roman times, galena is the principle ore of lead. It develops mineral-rich cubic crystals, which form when hot fluids find their way to higher levels in the Earth's crust.

HARDNESS	2.5
SG	7.6
COLOR	Lead-gray
TRANSPARENCY	Opaque
LUSTER	Metallic

Sphalerite

Sphalerite can occur in several different forms and is often mistaken for galena. This sulfide is an important source of zinc and can also be used as a gemstone.

HARDNESS	3–4
SG	3.9–4.1
COLOR	Brown, black, yellow
TRANSPARENCY	Opaque to transparent
LUSTER	Resinous to diamondlike, metallic

Acanthite

Occurring as spiked crystals, acanthite takes its name from the Greek word *akantha*, meaning "thorn." This sulfide is the main source of silver.

HARDNESS	2–2.5	**SG**	7.2–7.4
COLOR	Black		
TRANSPARENCY	Opaque		
LUSTER	Metallic		

Bornite

Known as "peacock ore" because of its iridescent splash of colors, bornite is a source of copper. Bornite crystals are rarely found as it usually occurs as massive aggregates.

HARDNESS	3	**SG**	5.1
COLOR	Coppery red, brown		
TRANSPARENCY	Opaque		
LUSTER	Metallic		

Covellite

This sulfide of copper is named after the Italian Nicolas Covelli, who first described it. It was first collected and identified at Mount Vesuvius, near Naples, Italy. When heated, covellite produces a blue-colored flame.

HARDNESS	1.5–2
SG	4.6–4.7
COLOR	Indigo-blue to black
TRANSPARENCY	Opaque
LUSTER	Submetallic to resinous

Pentlandite

Named after Irish scientist Joseph Pentland, pentlandite is a major ore of nickel. Nickel ores need extensive refining for releasing the metal. Deposits have been found in Canada and Russia, and also in meteorites.

HARDNESS	3.5–4
SG	4.6–5
COLOR	Bronze-yellow
TRANSPARENCY	Opaque
LUSTER	Metallic

Cinnabar

Highly poisonous, cinnabar is the main ore of mercury. It is the central ingredient in the pigment vermilion, and its brilliant orange-red color was used in paintings in ancient China. Cinnabar often forms around volcanic vents and hot springs.

HARDNESS	2–2.5	**SG**	8
COLOR	Red		
TRANSPARENCY	Transparent to opaque		
LUSTER	Diamondlike to dull		

Greenockite

This mineral is a cadmium ore, which is used for plating steel and other metals that get corroded easily. It is mixed with nickel to make rechargeable batteries.

HARDNESS 3–3.5 **SG** 4.8–4.9

COLOR Yellow, orange, orange-yellow, red

TRANSPARENCY Nearly opaque to translucent

LUSTER Resinous or diamondlike

Greenockite coating

Pyrrhotite

This magnetic mineral is a mixture of iron and sulfur in varying amounts. The amount of iron affects its magnetic properties. The mineral name is derived from the Greek word *pyrrhos*, which means "flame-colored."

HARDNESS 3.5–4.5 **SG** 4.6–4.7

COLOR Bronze-yellow to copper bronze-red

TRANSPARENCY Opaque

LUSTER Metallic

Realgar

After handling realgar, it's important to wash your hands because of the arsenic content.

Characterized by its bright red crystals, realgar has been used in Chinese art and for making fireworks. However, when exposed to light, the crystals crumble and form a yellow crust. Realgar is an important ore of the poison arsenic and is itself poisonous.

HARDNESS	1.5–2	**SG**	3.6
COLOR	Scarlet to orange-yellow		
TRANSPARENCY	Subtransparent to opaque		
LUSTER	Resinous to greasy		

Chalcocite

One of the most important ores of copper, chalcocite crystals were mined in Cornwall, England, for centuries. Copper is used for making aircraft and for other commercial and domestic purposes.

HARDNESS	2.5–3
SG	5.5–5.8
COLOR	Blackish lead-gray
TRANSPARENCY	Opaque
LUSTER	Metallic

Stannite

Stannite, an ore of tin, is found at Zeehan in Tasmania, Australia, and Cornwall in England. It occurs in tin-bearing, hydrothermal veins and rarely forms crystals.

HARDNESS	4	**SG**	4.4
COLOR	Steel-gray to iron-black		
TRANSPARENCY	Opaque		
LUSTER	Metallic		

Chalcopyrite

Though not very rich in copper, its widespread occurrence makes chalcopyrite an important copper ore. It is commonly found in hydrothermal ore veins deposited at high and medium temperatures.

HARDNESS	3.5–4
SG	4.2
COLOR	Brass-yellow
TRANSPARENCY	Opaque
LUSTER	Metallic

Stibnite

Stibnite's long, prism-shaped crystals have an unusual property—they can grow twisted and bent. Stibnite is the main ore of antimony, which is used for hardening lead and is added to paint and plastics as a flame-retardant.

HARDNESS 2   **SG** 4.6
COLOR Lead-gray to steel-gray, black
TRANSPARENCY Opaque
LUSTER Metallic

Prismlike crystals

In ancient times, powdered stibnite was used as makeup to darken eyelashes and eyebrows.

Millerite

This sulfide is an ore of nickel, used in metal alloys. It forms in needlelike crystals or in masses. It normally forms at low temperatures in holes in limestone or dolomite rocks, and is also found in meteorites. Millerite is named after English mineralogist W. H. Miller, who first studied it.

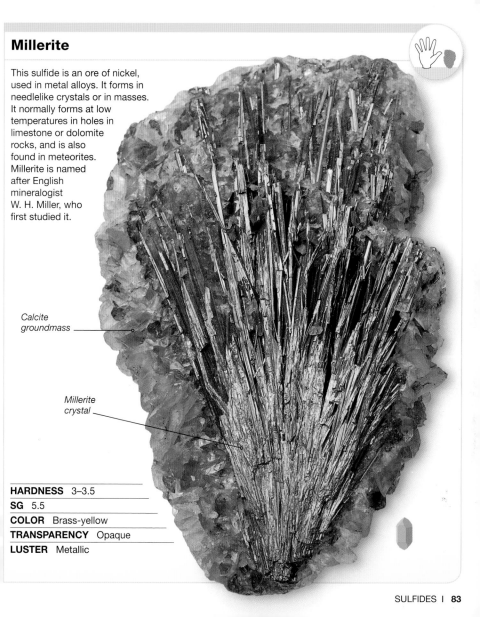

Calcite groundmass

Millerite crystal

HARDNESS	3–3.5
SG	5.5
COLOR	Brass-yellow
TRANSPARENCY	Opaque
LUSTER	Metallic

Orpiment

Orpiment takes its name from the Latin *auri pigmentum*, meaning "golden paint." Pigment derived from it was used in 19th-century paintings. However, it contains arsenic, which is poisonous.

HARDNESS 1.5–2	**SG** 3.5

COLOR Yellow

TRANSPARENCY Transparent to translucent

LUSTER Resinous

Pyrite

Bismuthinite

This rare mineral is a source of bismuth. When bismuth is mixed with other metals, it has a low melting point and is used in fire-safety devices, such as sprinkler heads.

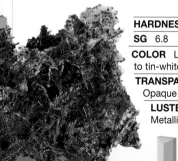

HARDNESS 2

SG 6.8

COLOR Lead-gray to tin-white

TRANSPARENCY Opaque

LUSTER Metallic

Marcasite

In the late Victorian era, marcasite was used to make mourning jewelry, worn at funeral ceremonies and other somber occasions. Its crystals tend to darken with exposure to air.

HARDNESS 6–6.5

SG 4.9

COLOR Pale bronze-yellow

TRANSPARENCY Opaque

LUSTER Metallic

Chalk groundmass

Also called fool's gold, pyrite was often mistaken for gold because of its brassy color and high density. Pyrite gets its name from Greek *pyr*, meaning "fire," because it emits sparks when struck by iron.

Cubic habit

HARDNESS	6–6.5
SG	5
COLOR	Pale brass-yellow
TRANSPARENCY	Opaque
LUSTER	Metallic

Hauerite

This manganese sulfide occurs in areas with salt deposits. It is found in Texas, the Ural Mountains of Russia, and Sicily, Italy.

HARDNESS	4
SG	3.5
COLOR	Red-brown to brown-black
TRANSPARENCY	Opaque
LUSTER	Diamondlike to submetallic

Cobaltite

Also known as cobalt glance, cobaltite is a source of cobalt. Cobalt is mixed with metals to make machine parts stronger and heat-resistant.

HARDNESS	5.5
SG	6.3
COLOR	Silver-white, pink
TRANSPARENCY	Opaque
LUSTER	Metallic

Arsenopyrite

This mineral is found in metamorphic and igneous rocks, in ore veins that form at moderate to high temperatures. It is the main source of arsenic and the most common of the minerals that contain this poison.

HARDNESS 5.5–6	**SG** 6.1
COLOR Silver-white to steel-gray	
TRANSPARENCY Opaque	
LUSTER Metallic	

Crystals are marked with grooves

When heated or struck, arsenopyrite gives off an odor that smells like garlic.

Molybdenite

This sulfide was originally mistaken for lead and so its name came from the Greek word for lead, *molybdos*. When added to alloys, it increases the hardness of iron and steel, protecting them against corrosion.

HARDNESS 1–1.5	**SG** 4.7
COLOR Lead-gray	
TRANSPARENCY Opaque	
LUSTER Metallic	

Sylvanite

Sylvanite is often found in small quantities in gold and silver deposits. It is photosensitive, which means it reacts to light, and can acquire a dark tarnish if exposed to bright light for too long.

HARDNESS 1–2	**SG** 8.2
COLOR Silver-white to pale yellow	
TRANSPARENCY Opaque	
LUSTER Metallic	

Chalcocite is one of the most important sources
of copper, which is the oldest metal known to man.
Copper is mainly obtained by smelting and refining.
Smelting usually involves heat and a chemical to
extract copper from its ore.

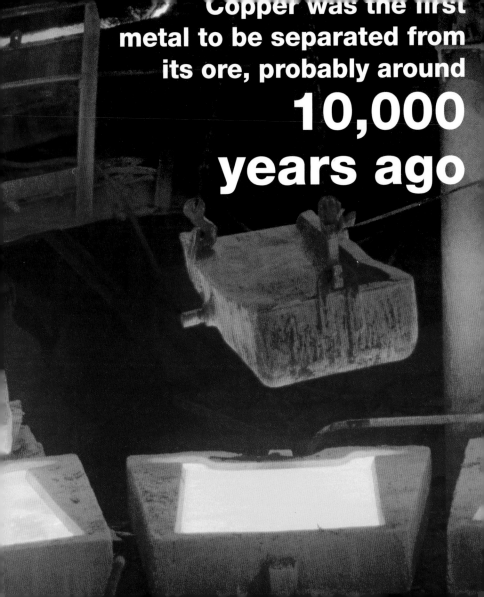

Copper was the first metal to be separated from its ore, probably around

10,000 years ago

FOCUS ON...
SITES
There are several sites across the world that are known for their sources of sulfosalts.

Sulfosalts

Sulfosalts are a large group of mostly rare minerals in which sulfur combines with a metal and a nonmetal. They have a luster similar to that of a metal and are dense and brittle.

▲ The Giant Mountains in the Czech Republic are a key site for polybasite and proustite.

▲ Jamesonite and atennantite are found in abundance in Chihuahua, Mexico.

▲ The Harz Mountains in Germany are a source of many sulfosalts, such as bournonite, boulangerite, and zinkenite.

Tetrahedrite

Tetrahedrite is an important ore of copper and has been mined all over the world for centuries. It is also sometimes mined for its silver content. Austria, Germany, England, Mexico, and Peru are some of the important sites for tetrahedrite.

HARDNESS	3–4
SG	4.6–5.1
COLOR	Flint-gray to iron-black
TRANSPARENCY	Opaque
LUSTER	Metallic

Pyrargyrite

Pyrargyrite is an important source of silver. Also called dark ruby silver, it darkens when exposed to light. Its name derives from the Greek words *pyr,* meaning "fire," and *argent*, meaning "silver."

HARDNESS 2.5	SG 5.8
COLOR Deep red	
TRANSPARENCY Translucent	
LUSTER Diamondlike	

Proustite

Proustite is sensitive to light and turns from transparent scarlet to opaque gray when exposed to strong light. Its bright wine-red crystals make attractive gems. Chile and Germany are notable sources of this mineral.

HARDNESS 2–2.5
SG 5.8
COLOR Scarlet, gray
TRANSPARENCY Translucent
LUSTER Diamondlike to submetallic

Bournonite

A combination of copper, lead, antimony, and sulfur, bournonite forms tablet-shaped prismatic crystals. Some of the crystals found in the mineral-rich Harz Mountains of Germany have a diameter of 1 in (2.5 cm) or more. It has been nicknamed "cogwheel ore," since it sometimes develops crystals in the shape of a cogwheel.

HARDNESS 2.5–3
SG 5.8
COLOR Steel-gray
TRANSPARENCY Opaque
LUSTER Metallic

Oxides

These minerals form when oxygen combines with a metal or semimetal. In simple oxides, only a single metal or semimetal is present, but multiple oxides may contain several.

FOCUS ON...
MAJOR ORES
Some minerals are mined as ores as they contain useful elements such as metals.

Ruby

Known in Sanskrit as *ratnaraj* or "king of precious stones," ruby is the red variety of corundum, the hardest mineral on the Earth after diamond. Heating improves its color and clarity. Crystals of ruby tend to be small, since the presence of chromium hampers their growth. Therefore, large rubies have high value. Several myths and beliefs are associated with ruby. In Burmese tradition, ruby bestows good fortune and invincibility, and Russians traditionally consider it to be good for the heart, brain, blood purification, and vitality.

HARDNESS 9	**SG** 4–4.1
COLOR Red	

TRANSPARENCY
Transparent to translucent

LUSTER Diamondlike to glassy

▲ The mineral cuprite is an ore of copper—which is widely used for making electrical wires.

▲ Chromite is a significant source of the metal chromium. It is mixed with steel when manufacturing stainless steel.

▲ Titanium, which comes from rutile, is very strong and is used in aircraft, spacecraft, missiles, and ships.

Sapphire

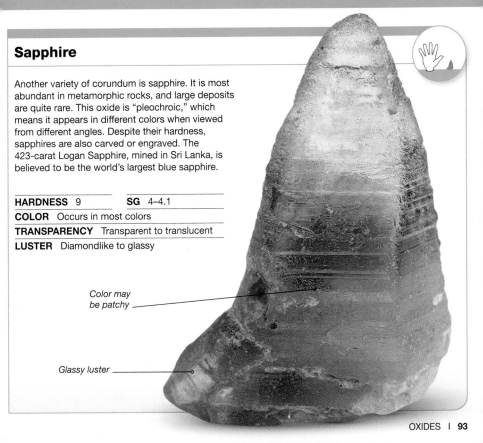

Another variety of corundum is sapphire. It is most abundant in metamorphic rocks, and large deposits are quite rare. This oxide is "pleochroic," which means it appears in different colors when viewed from different angles. Despite their hardness, sapphires are also carved or engraved. The 423-carat Logan Sapphire, mined in Sri Lanka, is believed to be the world's largest blue sapphire.

HARDNESS 9	SG 4–4.1
COLOR Occurs in most colors	
TRANSPARENCY Transparent to translucent	
LUSTER Diamondlike to glassy	

Color may be patchy

Glassy luster

Magnetite

This mineral is so highly magnetic, it will attract iron and can move a compass needle. The ancient Chinese made their first compasses with magnetite.

HARDNESS	5.5–6	SG	5.2

COLOR Black to brownish-black

TRANSPARENCY Opaque

LUSTER Metallic to semimetallic

Spinel

The red variety of this mineral is hard and is cut as a gemstone. It looks similar to ruby—the Black Prince's Ruby in the British Imperial State Crown was found to be a spinel.

HARDNESS	7.5–8	SG	3.6

COLOR Red, yellow, orange-red, blue, green, brown, black

TRANSPARENCY Transparent to translucent

LUSTER Glassy

Cassiterite

A tin oxide, cassiterite derives its name from *kassiteros*, the Greek word for "tin". It is a major source of tin and is found in China, Malaysia, and Indonesia.

HARDNESS	6–7	SG	7

COLOR Medium to dark brown

TRANSPARENCY Transparent to opaque

LUSTER Diamondlike to metallic

Zincite

Also known as red oxide of zinc, zincite rarely forms crystals. It is found in Sterling Hill, New Jersey.

Zincite

HARDNESS	4

SG 5.7

COLOR Orange-yellow to deep red

TRANSPARENCY Almost opaque

LUSTER Resinous

Chromite

Chromite is the major source of chromium. This metal is mixed with iron to make high-speed tools and stainless steel.

HARDNESS 5.5 **SG** 4.7

COLOR Dark brown, black

TRANSPARENCY Opaque

LUSTER Metallic

Chrysoberyl

This mineral has been used in Asia for thousands of years as an amulet to protect against "the evil eye." Its gemstone variety, alexandrite, is one of the rarest and most expensive gems.

HARDNESS 8.5

SG 3.7

COLOR
Green, yellow

TRANSPARENCY
Transparent to translucent

LUSTER Glassy

Hematite

Hematite is the most important ore of iron. Its name is derived from the Greek *haimatitis*, meaning "blood-red"—a reference to the red color of its powder. It has long been associated with blood—bones of Neolithic burials have been found smeared with hematite powder.

HARDNESS 5–6 **SG** 5.3

COLOR Steel-gray

TRANSPARENCY
Opaque

LUSTER
Metallic
to dull

Perovskite

Found in the Earth's upper mantle, Perovskite was first discovered in the Ural Mountains of Russia.

HARDNESS
5.5

SG 4

COLOR Black, brown, yellow

TRANSPARENCY
Transparent to opaque

LUSTER
Diamondlike, metallic

Uraninite

A radioactive mineral, uraninite is the main source of uranium, which is used to power nuclear reactors. In earlier times, it was used in small amounts for coloring ceramics.

HARDNESS 5–6 **SG** 6.5–11
COLOR Black to brownish-black, dark gray, greenish
TRANSPARENCY Opaque
LUSTER Submetallic, pitchy, dull

Samarskite

Named after Russian mining engineer Vasili Samarski-Bykhovets, samarskite contains uranium and has radioactive crystals. It was discovered in Miass, Russia.

HARDNESS 5–6 **SG** 5.7
COLOR Black
TRANSPARENCY Translucent to opaque
LUSTER Glassy to resinous

Brookite

This mineral is named after English crystallographer H. J. Brooke. It is one of the few naturally occurring polymorphs (a mineral that can crystallize in different forms).

HARDNESS 5.5–6 **SG** 4.1
COLOR Various shades of brown
TRANSPARENCY Opaque to transparent
LUSTER Metallic to diamondlike

Brookite

Pyrochlore

This mineral gets its name from Greek words for "fire" and "green" because it turns green after heating. It is an important source of niobium, a soft gray metal used mostly in alloys such as steel.

HARDNESS	5–5.5
SG	4.5
COLOR Brown to black	
TRANSPARENCY Translucent to opaque	
LUSTER Glassy to resinous	

Albite

Rutile

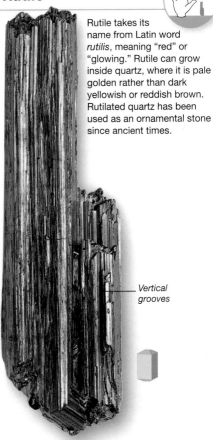

Rutile takes its name from Latin word *rutilis*, meaning "red" or "glowing." Rutile can grow inside quartz, where it is pale golden rather than dark yellowish or reddish brown. Rutilated quartz has been used as an ornamental stone since ancient times.

Vertical grooves

HARDNESS 6–6.5		**SG** 4.2
COLOR Reddish-brown to red		
TRANSPARENCY Transparent to opaque		
LUSTER Diamondlike to submetallic		

Hydroxides

Hydroxides form when a metal combines with water and oxygen at a low temperature. They are usually found in sedimentary rocks and are often important ore minerals. Many hydroxide minerals are very soft.

Diaspore

Diaspore takes its name from the Greek word for "scatter", because when it is heated, it crackles and scatters light. This makes it look as though it has different colors when seen from different angles.

HARDNESS	6.5–7	SG	3.4

COLOR White, gray, yellow, lilac, or pink

TRANSPARENCY Transparent to translucent

LUSTER Glassy

Bauxite

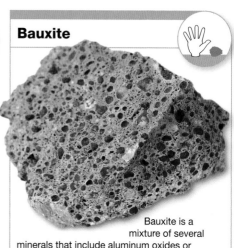

Bauxite is a mixture of several minerals that include aluminum oxides or hydroxides. Technically it is a rock, but it's usually grouped with minerals. It is an important source of aluminum. Of all the bauxite mined, 90 percent is used to extract aluminum.

HARDNESS	1–3	SG	2.3–2.7

COLOR White, yellowish, red, reddish-brown

TRANSPARENCY Opaque

LUSTER Earthy

Goethite

German poet and author Johann Wolfgang von Goethe was an enthusiastic mineralogist, and goethite is named after him. It is an iron oxide hydroxide and can occur as grooved crystals.

HARDNESS	5–5.5
SG	4.3
COLOR	Orangish to blackish-brown
TRANSPARENCY	Translucent to opaque
LUSTER	Diamondlike to metallic

Limonite

Limonite has been used as a pigment in painting since ancient Egyptian times, and was also used by the Dutch portrait artist Anthony van Dyck. It forms as a secondary mineral when other minerals oxidize (react with oxygen) and doesn't form crystals.

HARDNESS	4–5.5
SG	2.7–4.3
COLOR	Various shades of brown, yellow
TRANSPARENCY	Opaque
LUSTER	Earthy, sometimes submetallic or dull

Many halides can be found in our homes and are used on a daily basis.

▲ Cryolite is used in the production of aluminum, which gives us aluminum foil.

▲ Halite, or common salt, is used as a preservative and as seasoning in foods.

▲ Fluorine, from fluorite, is used to give some cooking pans a nonstick surface.

Halides

Halides are soft minerals and have a low specific gravity. These minerals form when metals combine with one of the common halogen elements, which include fluorine, chlorine, bromine, and iodine.

Halite

Halite is common edible salt, or sodium chloride. A vital mineral for human and animal health, salt is also used as a preservative and in making soap and glass. Halite forms as salty deposits when saltwater evaporates, and is found worldwide.

HARDNESS 2.5	**SG** 2.1–2.6
COLOR Colorless to white	
TRANSPARENCY Transparent to translucent	
LUSTER Glassy	

Fluorite

Fluorite melts easily, and its name comes from the Latin *fluere*, "to flow." When seen under ultraviolet light, this mineral is fluorescent (it gives off a glowing light).

HARDNESS 4   **SG** 3.2–3.6

COLOR Occurs in most colors

TRANSPARENCY Transparent to translucent

LUSTER Glassy

Cryolite

Molten cryolite was mixed with aluminum oxides for the manufacture of aircraft and engineering products.

HARDNESS 2.5   **SG** 3

COLOR Colorless to snow-white

TRANSPARENCY Transparent to translucent

LUSTER Glassy to greasy

Carnallite

Carnallite forms when potassium and magnesium chloride mix with water. It is an important source of the chemical potash.

HARDNESS 2.5   **SG** 1.6

COLOR Milky white, often reddish

TRANSPARENCY Translucent to opaque

LUSTER Greasy

Atacamite

The Statue of Liberty in New York City is colored green by a layer of atacamite. The mineral is named for the Atacama Desert in Chile.

HARDNESS 3–3.5   **SG** 3.8

COLOR Bright green to blackish-green

TRANSPARENCY Transparent to translucent

LUSTER Diamondlike to glassy

The world's largest salt flat, Salar de Uyuni contains around

10 billion

tons of salt

HALITE
Large crystals of halite, or common salt, forms after the evaporation of water from the sea or saltwater lakes. Salar de Uyuni, in Bolivia, is the remains of a prehistoric salt lake. It covers an area of 4,086 sq miles (10,582 sq km).

Carbonates

Carbonate minerals form when a carbonate (carbon and oxygen) combines with metals or semimetals. They can be found in sea shells, coral reefs, and rocks such as marble and chalk.

FOCUS ON...
CALCITE
Most carbonates found in the Earth's crust are calcite—a useful form of calcium carbonate.

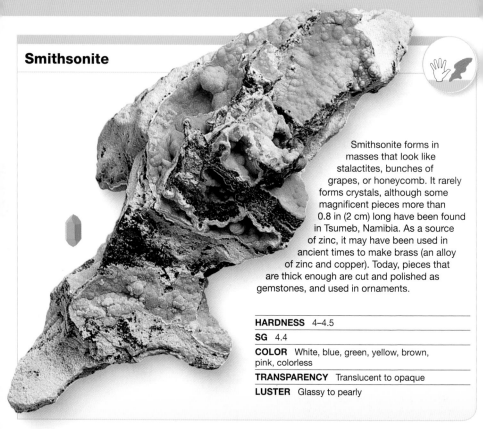

Smithsonite

Smithsonite forms in masses that look like stalactites, bunches of grapes, or honeycomb. It rarely forms crystals, although some magnificent pieces more than 0.8 in (2 cm) long have been found in Tsumeb, Namibia. As a source of zinc, it may have been used in ancient times to make brass (an alloy of zinc and copper). Today, pieces that are thick enough are cut and polished as gemstones, and used in ornaments.

HARDNESS	4–4.5
SG	4.4
COLOR	White, blue, green, yellow, brown, pink, colorless
TRANSPARENCY	Translucent to opaque
LUSTER	Glassy to pearly

▲ White and yellow calcite was quarried in ancient Egypt and used in buildings and statues.

▲ Marble is another form of calcite. Strong and decorative, it is still used in buildings today.

▲ Found inside caves, calcite forms long, thin stalactites that build up as water drips.

▲ Calcium carbonate taken from calcite is the main ingredient for indigestion tablets.

Calcite

One of the three most common carbonates on the Earth, this calcium carbonate grows anywhere that water can reach. Shellfish make their shells from calcite, which they take from seawater. Calcite is known for its beautiful crystals, and although it can be almost any color, in its pure form it is white or colorless.

HARDNESS 3

SG 2.7

COLOR Colorless, white, yellow, black, green

TRANSPARENCY Transparent to translucent

LUSTER Glassy

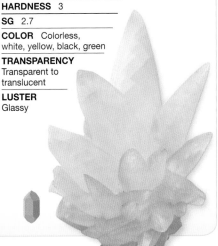

Siderite

This shiny mineral is an iron carbonate and takes its name from the Greek *sideros,* meaning "iron." Its crystals often have curved faces. When heated, siderite becomes magnetic.

HARDNESS 3.5–4 **SG** 3.9

COLOR Yellowish-brown to dark brown

TRANSPARENCY Translucent

LUSTER Glassy to pearly

Aragonite

Formed at low temperatures near the Earth's surface, aragonite is found in caves and around hot springs. It forms different shapes, including one that resembles coral. In this shape it is called *flos-ferri*, meaning "flowers of iron."

HARDNESS	3.5–4
SG	2.9
COLOR	Colorless, white, gray, yellowish, reddish, green
TRANSPARENCY	Transparent to translucent
LUSTER	Glassy inclining to resinous

Malachite

Malachite is possibly one of the oldest known sources of copper. In ancient Egypt, it was used as an eye paint, probably to prevent eye infections.

HARDNESS	3.5–4	**SG**	3.9–4
COLOR	Bright green		
TRANSPARENCY	Translucent		
LUSTER	Diamondlike to silky		

Rhodochrosite

Gem-quality crystals of this manganese carbonate can be found in the United States and South Africa. These are sometimes cut for collectors. The more common form has a band of colors and is used as decorative stone.

The Incas believed that rhodochrosite was the blood of ancient kings and queens that had turned to stone.

Aurichalcite

Aurichalcite is Latin for "golden copper." It has a distinctive velvetlike coating. It burns with a green flame because it contains copper.

HARDNESS 1–2   **SG** 4.2
COLOR Sky-blue, green-blue, or pale green
TRANSPARENCY Transparent to translucent
LUSTER Silky to pearly

Ankerite

Harder than a piece of copper, but softer than steel, ankerite forms distinctive curved crystals. It is a rare mineral and is not mined for any specific purpose.

HARDNESS 3.5–4   **SG** 2.9
COLOR Colorless to pale buff
TRANSPARENCY Translucent
LUSTER Glassy to pearly

HARDNESS 3.5–4   **SG** 3.8
COLOR Rose-pink, brown or gray
TRANSPARENCY Transparent to translucent
LUSTER Glassy to pearly

Barytocalcite

This mineral is made up of barium and calcite. Its surface is covered in grooves and ridges that look like dog's teeth. It is often found within limestone and produces bubbles when put in hydrochloric acid.

HARDNESS 4	**SG** 3.7

COLOR White, grayish, greenish, or yellowish

TRANSPARENCY Transparent to translucent

LUSTER Glassy to resinous

Dolomite

This common mineral is recognized by its curved saddle-shaped crystals. It is an important rock-forming mineral and also a minor source of magnesium.

HARDNESS 3.5-4

SG 2.8-2.9

COLOR Colorless, white, or cream

TRANSPARENCY Transparent to translucent

LUSTER Glassy

Magnesite

It is almost impossible to melt magnesite, making it ideal for lining furnaces. It is also used in the production of synthetic rubber.

HARDNESS 4

SG 3

COLOR White, light gray, yellowish, brownish

TRANSPARENCY Transparent to translucent

LUSTER Glassy

Phosgenite

This rare carbonate forms close to the Earth's surface when lead-rich minerals react with water. It is named after the colorless and poisonous gas phosgene, since they are both made up of carbon, oxygen, and chlorine.

HARDNESS 2.5–3	**SG** 6.1

COLOR White, yellow, brown, or green

TRANSPARENCY Transparent to translucent

LUSTER Resinous

Azurite

Azurite takes its name from the Persian *lazhudward*, meaning "blue." In the 15th to 17th centuries, it was used as a natural coloring pigment in European art. It is also one of the sources of copper.

HARDNESS 3.5–4

SG 3.8

COLOR
Azure to dark blue

TRANSPARENCY
Transparent to translucent

LUSTER
Glassy to dull to earthy

Artinite

Artinite forms fluffy balls of needle-shaped crystals. It dissolves in cold acids, giving off water and carbon dioxide.

HARDNESS 2.5   **SG** 2

COLOR White

TRANSPARENCY
Transparent

LUSTER
Glassy

Small radiating crystal

Strontianite

The crystals of this mineral are short, columnar, and needle-shaped. It is the main source of strontium and is used in sugar refining for extracting sugar from sugarcane.

HARDNESS 3.5–4   **SG** 3.7

COLOR Colorless, gray, green, yellow, or reddish

TRANSPARENCY
Transparent to translucent

LUSTER
Glassy

Trona

Trona takes it name from the Arabic *natrun*, meaning "salt." It is usually found on the surface of the Earth in powdery form, especially in dry, salty desert areas. It is also a source of sodium.

HARDNESS 2.5–3   **SG** 2.1

COLOR Colorless to gray, yellow-white

TRANSPARENCY Transparent to translucent

LUSTER Glassy, glistening

Phosphates, arsenates, and vanadates

These minerals are grouped together because they have similar patterns of atoms. The most abundant of the three are phosphates, with more than 200 known types.

Variscite

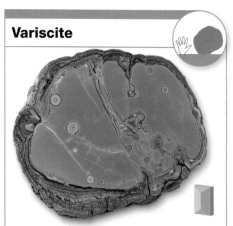

This mineral is named after Varisca, the old name for the German district of Voightland where variscite was first found. It is sometimes worn as jewelry, but it is porous and can absorb the body's natural oils, which discolor it.

HARDNESS 4.5		**SG** 2.6	
COLOR Pale to apple-green			
TRANSPARENCY Opaque			
LUSTER Glassy to waxy			

Pyromorphite

A minor ore of lead, this phosphate occurs in the oxidized zone of lead deposits. Pyromorphite gets its name from the Greek word *pyr*, meaning "fire," and *morphe*, meaning "form." It is so named because it forms crystals on cooling after being melted.

HARDNESS 3.5–4		**SG** 7	
COLOR Green, yellow, orange, or brown			
TRANSPARENCY Transparent to translucent			
LUSTER Resinous			

Wavellite

Radiating crystal

Wavellite contains a mixture of oxygen, aluminum, and phosphorus. It forms balls of crystals in chert rock, limestone, and granite. When these balls are broken, they reveal disklike patterns.

HARDNESS 3.5–4	SG 2.4
COLOR Green or white	
TRANSPARENCY Translucent	
LUSTER Glassy to resinous	

Turquoise

One of the first gemstones to be mined, turquoise varies from sky-blue to green, depending on the amount of iron or copper in it. Turquoise was the national gemstone of Persia (now Iran). The Persians believed that seeing the reflection of a new Moon on a turquoise stone brought good luck.

HARDNESS 5–6	SG 2.6–2.8
COLOR Blue, green	
TRANSPARENCY Usually opaque	
LUSTER Waxy to dull	

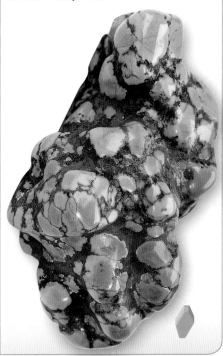

Apatite

Apatite is a name given to a group of minerals that contain calcium and phosphorus. It is used to make many things, including matches. Apatite derives its name from the Greek word *apate,* which means "deceit," because it looks similar to other minerals, including amethyst, aquamarine, and olivine.

HARDNESS	5

SG 3.1–3.2

COLOR Green, blue, violet, purple, colorless, yellow, or rose

TRANSPARENCY Transparent to translucent

LUSTER Glassy, waxy

Carnotite

A radioactive mineral, carnotite is an important source of uranium and gives off radium gas.

HARDNESS 2	**SG** 4.7

COLOR Yellow

TRANSPARENCY Semitransparent to opaque

LUSTER Pearly to dull

Chalcophyllite

This mineral is named after the Greek words for "copper" and "leaf" because it contains copper and grows in a leaflike pattern. Easy to mold, copper has been cast since 4,000 BCE.

HARDNESS 2	**SG** 2.7

COLOR Vivid blue-green

TRANSPARENCY Transparent to translucent

LUSTER Pearly to glassy

Adamite

This mineral is generally highly fluorescent—when viewed under ultraviolet light, it gives off amazing colors. It has no commercial use but its bright and lustrous crystals are sought by mineral collectors.

HARDNESS 3.5	**SG** 4.4
	COLOR Yellow, green, pink or violet
	TRANSPARENCY Transparent to translucent
	LUSTER Glassy

Erythrite

This brightly colored mineral is commonly called cobalt bloom. It is an ore of cobalt, nickel, and silver. Some of the best erythrite is found in Canada and Morocco.

HARDNESS 1.5–2.5

SG 3.1

COLOR Purple-pink

TRANSPARENCY Transparent to translucent

LUSTER Diamondlike to glassy, pearly

Mimetite

Mimetite deposits are found where lead and arsenic occur together. Its name is derived from the Greek *mimetes*, meaning "imitator," because of its resemblance to pyromorphite.

HARDNESS 3.5–4

SG 7.3

COLOR Pale yellow to yellowish-brown, orange, green

TRANSPARENCY Subtransparent

LUSTER Resinous

This Aztec funeral mask is made of turquoise, gold, and shell overlaid on a

human

skull

Borax is the main source of boron, which is used in the manufacture of many essential products.

▲ Boron is added to many fertilizers, since it helps plants to grow.

◀ Boron is one of the ingredients in some mouthwashes. It is also used as a disinfectant.

▲ Boron compounds from borax are an important component of many soaps.

Nitrates and borates

These minerals are formed when oxygen combines with nitrogen and boron respectively. They have low specific gravity and are usually soft.

Borax

The name borax comes from the Arabic *buraq*, which means "white." It is an evaporite mineral that forms in large desert lake beds, and contains sodium and boron. Borax can fuse or melt easily to become colorless glass, and is also a source of boron.

HARDNESS 2–2.5	**SG** 1.7
COLOR Colorless	
TRANSPARENCY Transparent to translucent	
LUSTER Glassy to earthy	

Howlite

Howlite is named after its discoverer, Canadian chemist Henry How. It can be dyed and used in place of turquoise, although it is not as hard as turquoise and lacks depth of color. Significant deposits of howlite are found in Death Valley, California.

HARDNESS 3.5	**SG** 2.6

COLOR White

TRANSPARENCY Translucent to opaque

LUSTER Almost glassy

Nitratine

Found in arid areas as a powderlike deposit on the Earth's surface, nitratine is easily soluble in water and readily absorbs moisture from the air. It occurs mainly as huge grains and in crusts.

HARDNESS 1.5–2

SG 2.27

COLOR White or colorless

TRANSPARENCY Transparent

LUSTER Glassy

Sulfates, chromates, molybdates, tungstates

Oxygen combines with sulfur, chromium, molybdenum, and tungsten respectively to form these minerals. In their concentrated form they are valuable ores of the metal or semimetal they contain.

Crocoite

Crocoite takes its name from the Greek word for "saffron," which is a reference to its brilliant color. However, it loses its sheen when exposed to light. Fine crocoite specimens are found in Tasmania, Australia, and it is the official mineral emblem of the island.

HARDNESS	2.5–3
SG	6
COLOR	Orange, red
TRANSPARENCY	Transparent to translucent
LUSTER	Glassy

FOCUS ON...
GYPSUM

This common sulfate is widely used, especially in building and design.

▲ Gypsum is used for making plaster of Paris and mortar and also as an adhesive in industrial processes.

▲ Alabaster, a fine-grained form of gypsum, is used for carvings and ornamental purposes.

Wulfenite

Named after mineralogist F. X. Wulfen, this mineral is often found with lead ores and is a minor source of molybdenum. Its unique square-shaped crystals look like interlocking plastic tiles. Large crystals come from Mexico, the United States, Zambia, China, and Slovenia.

HARDNESS 2.5–3		**SG** 6.5–7
COLOR Yellow, orange, red		
TRANSPARENCY Transparent to translucent		
LUSTER Diamondlike to greasy		

Ferberite

Ferberite is named after German mineralogist Dr. Moritz Rudolph Ferber. It is an iron tungstate that usually occurs as flat, stepped crystals, and is an ore of tungsten. This very useful metal is used in electric-light filaments.

HARDNESS	4–4.5	SG	7.5

COLOR Black

TRANSPARENCY Opaque

LUSTER Submetallic

Chalcanthite

Gypsum

Gypsum is formed when seawater evaporates. Such surface-forming minerals are usually soft. An extremely common substance, gypsum is mined on a large scale in many parts of the world. Plaster of Paris, alabaster, fertilizers, and some types of explosives contain gypsum.

HARDNESS	2	SG	2.3

COLOR Colorless, white, light brown, yellow, pink

TRANSPARENCY Transparent to translucent

LUSTER Almost glassy to pearly

Chalcanthite dissolves easily in water and is, therefore, more common in dry regions. It used to be known as blue vitriol, but is now named for the Greek words for "copper" and "flower." It is an important ore of copper especially in dry regions such as Chile.

HARDNESS	2.5
SG	2.3
COLOR	Blue
TRANSPARENCY	Transparent
LUSTER	Glassy

Brochantite

This mineral is named after French geologist A. J. M. Brochant de Villiers. It is a source of copper. The needlelike crystals of brochantite are a few millimeters long, but magnificent specimens ½ in (1 cm) long are found in Namibia and Arizona.

HARDNESS	3.5–4	**SG**	4
COLOR	Emerald-green		
TRANSPARENCY	Translucent		
LUSTER	Glassy		

Scheelite

Opaque crystals of scheelite weighing up to 15 lb (7 kg) are found in Arizona. It is a major source of tungsten. The nozzle of the Saturn V rocket, which launched *Apollo 11* in 1969, was made of tungsten-steel.

HARDNESS	4.5–5	**SG**	6.1
COLOR	White, yellow, brown, green		
TRANSPARENCY	Transparent to translucent		
LUSTER	Glassy to greasy		

Baryte

Also known as heavy spar, this mineral gets its name from *barys,* the Greek word for "heavy," because it has a high specific gravity. It is the main source of barium, and is used in oil and gas wells, in paper, and in cloth-making.

HARDNESS	3–3.5
SG	4.5
COLOR	Colorless, white, gray, bluish, greenish, beige
TRANSPARENCY	Transparent to translucent
LUSTER	Glassy, resinous, pearly

GEMSTONES
Several silicates are
used as gemstones
because of their
colorful crystals.

▶ Jade is a
tough mineral,
which makes
it ideal for
carving.

▲ Precious opal can form
only in undisturbed space
within another rock.

▲ The ancient Egyptians
believed that topaz was
colored in the glow of
the Sun god Ra.

Silicates

The biggest group of minerals, silicates
are found in abundance and are the main
components of igneous and metamorphic
rocks. Made of silicon and oxygen, they
are usually hard, transparent, and are
moderately dense.

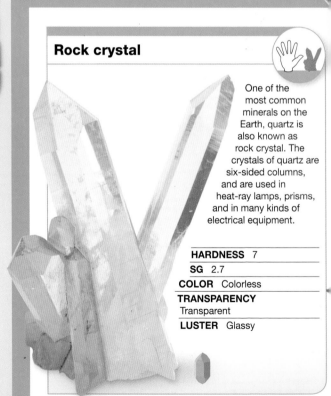

Rock crystal

One of the
most common
minerals on the
Earth, quartz is
also known as
rock crystal. The
crystals of quartz are
six-sided columns,
and are used in
heat-ray lamps, prisms,
and in many kinds of
electrical equipment.

HARDNESS	7
SG	2.7
COLOR	Colorless
TRANSPARENCY	Transparent
LUSTER	Glassy

Amethyst

Purple quartz is called amethyst, named after the maiden Amethyst from Greek mythology. Amethyst was very popular in 19th-century jewelry. Its color comes from tiny quantities of iron in it. Some amethyst crystals turn yellow-brown when heated. These are often sold as citrine.

HARDNESS	7
SG	2.7
COLOR	Violet
TRANSPARENCY	Opaque to translucent
LUSTER	Glassy

Citrine

The name citrine comes from the Latin word *citrina,* meaning "yellow." It gets its color from the iron oxide present in it. The mineral is also known as gold topaz.

HARDNESS	7
SG	2.7
COLOR	Yellow, yellow-brown
TRANSPARENCY	Translucent to nearly opaque
LUSTER	Glassy

Rose quartz

The pink variety of quartz is known as rose quartz. It has been carved since ancient times. Today, "crystal healers" believe that this mineral can bring unconditional love if worn against the skin.

HARDNESS	7	**SG**	2.65
COLOR Various, including pink and rose			
TRANSPARENCY Translucent to nearly opaque			
LUSTER Glassy			

Agate

Agate is the banded variety of chalcedony, a fine-grained quartz. It usually grows in rings around a common center, in rock cavities or extrusive igneous rocks.

HARDNESS 6.5–7	**SG** 2.6

COLOR Colorless, white, yellow, gray, brown, blue, or red

TRANSPARENCY Translucent to opaque

LUSTER Glassy to waxy

Bloodstone

According to ancient Greek lore, bloodstone was a preserver of health and offered protection against nosebleeds, anger, and discord. Bloodstones are named for their red spots, which resemble drops of blood.

HARDNESS 6.5–7	**SG** 2.6
	COLOR Different colors with red spots
	TRANSPARENCY Translucent to opaque
	LUSTER Glassy

Onyx

Onyx is the striped, semiprecious variety of agate with alternating bands of color. The layers of contrasting colors make it an ideal material for carving jewelry.

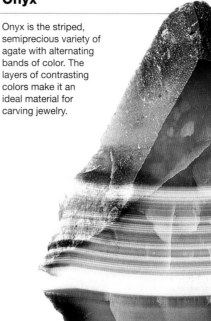

Translucent brown sard

HARDNESS 6.5–7

SG 2.6

COLOR Different colors

TRANSPARENCY Translucent to nearly opaque

LUSTER Glassy

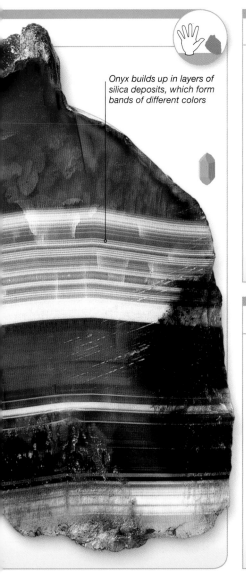

Onyx builds up in layers of silica deposits, which form bands of different colors

Opal

Opal occurs in many forms and many different crystal shapes. It is used as a semiprecious gemstone and is chiefly found in Australia.

HARDNESS 5–6	SG 1.9–2.3
COLOR Colorless, white, yellow, orange, rose-red, black, or dark blue	
TRANSPARENCY Transparent to translucent	
LUSTER Glassy	

Sard

A translucent mineral, sard has been used since ancient times for making cameos and jewelry. It was used at Harappa, one of the oldest centers of the Indus civilization (c. 2,300–1,500 BCE).

HARDNESS 6.5–7	SG 2.6
COLOR Light to dark-brown	
TRANSPARENCY Translucent to opaque	
LUSTER Glassy	

Lazurite

This rare mineral forms in limestone and it is the main mineral in lapis lazuli—a rock prized for its use in carvings, medicines, cosmetics, and jewelry for thousands of years. Lazurite is also the main ingredient of a brilliant blue pigment called ultramarine. The best lazurite crystals come from Afghanistan.

HARDNESS 5–5.5	**SG** 2.4

COLOR Various intense shades of blue

TRANSPARENCY Translucent to opaque

LUSTER Dull to glassy

Leucite

The Greek word *leukos*, meaning "white," gives leucite its name—a reference to its most common color. Leucite occurs only in igneous rocks, mainly those that are potassium-rich and silica-poor.

HARDNESS 5.5–6	**SG** 2.5

COLOR White, gray, or colorless

TRANSPARENCY Transparent to translucent

LUSTER Glassy

Leucite

Bedrock

Orthoclase

A major rock-forming mineral, orthoclase's pink crystals give granite its characteristic color. This mineral is important in ceramics, where it is used as a clay for making objects and as a glaze. Moonstone, the smooth and shiny variety of orthoclase, was regarded as sacred in India.

HARDNESS 6	SG 2.5–2.6

COLOR Colorless, white, cream, yellow, pink, brown-red

TRANSPARENCY Transparent to translucent

LUSTER Glassy

Cancrinite

This silicate was found originally in the Ural Mountains in Russia. It forms in a number of igneous rocks. Cancrinite rarely forms crystals, although they may grow to a few inches wide.

HARDNESS 5–6	SG 2.5

COLOR Pale to dark yellow, orange, violet, pink, or purple

TRANSPARENCY Transparent to translucent

LUSTER Glassy

Topaz

This mineral's name was probably inspired by the Sanskrit word *tapas*, which means "fire"—a reference to its golden-yellow color. Topaz also exists in other colors. It is classified as a gemstone because of its beautiful and rare crystals.

HARDNESS 8   **SG** 3.4–3.6

COLOR Colorless, blue, yellow, pink, brown, green

TRANSPARENCY Transparent to translucent

LUSTER Glassy

Grossular

Zircon

This mineral often matches diamond in its sparkling brilliance. Some crystals of zircon found in Mount Narryer in western Australia are almost 4.4 billion years old.

HARDNESS 7.5   **SG** 4.6–4.7

COLOR Colorless, brown, red, yellow, orange, blue, green

TRANSPARENCY Transparent to opaque

LUSTER Diamondlike to oily

Kyanite

This silicate has been used to make heat-resistant porcelains, such as used in spark plugs. Gem-quality kyanite crystals are found in Bahia, Brazil. Its name is an adaptation of the Greek word *kyanos*, meaning "dark blue"—a reference to one of its many color forms.

HARDNESS 4.5–6

SG 3.6

COLOR Blue, green

TRANSPARENCY Transparent to translucent

LUSTER Glassy

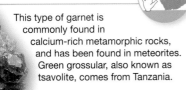

This type of garnet is commonly found in calcium-rich metamorphic rocks, and has been found in meteorites. Green grossular, also known as tsavolite, comes from Tanzania.

HARDNESS 6.5–7

SG 3.6

COLOR Wide range of colors

TRANSPARENCY Transparent to translucent

LUSTER Glassy

Andalusite

Andalusite is usually found in metamorphic rocks. Sometimes its crystals grow together trapping dark, carbon-based matter in between, which forms a cross when seen in cross-section.

HARDNESS 6.5–7.5   **SG** 3.2

COLOR Pink, brown, white, gray, violet, yellow, green, blue

TRANSPARENCY Transparent to nearly opaque

LUSTER Glassy

Sillimanite

This is named after Professor Benjamin Silliman, a geologist, chemist, and founder of the *American Journal of Science*. Sillimanite is commonly used to make heat-resistant porcelain.

HARDNESS 7

SG 3.2–3.3

COLOR Colorless, white, pale yellow, blue, green, violet

TRANSPARENCY Transparent to translucent

LUSTER Silky

Olivine

Olivine refers to a group of silicate minerals that form in molten rock beneath the Earth's surface. The ancient Greeks and Romans were among the first people to use these minerals for decoration. Peridot is the gem-quality variety of olivine.

HARDNESS 6.5–7	**SG** 3.3–4.3	
COLOR Green, yellow, brown, white, or black		
TRANSPARENCY Transparent to translucent		
LUSTER Glassy		

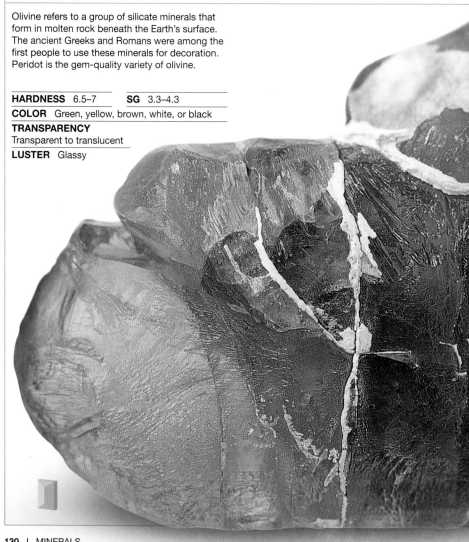

The gold throne in Topkapi Palace, Istanbul, is decorated with 955 peridots.

Natrolite

Natrolite takes its name from the Greek *natrium*, which means "soda"—a reference to its sodium content. It is found in cavities, volcanic ash deposits, and as veins in some rocks.

HARDNESS 5–5.5

SG 2.3

COLOR Pale pink, colorless, white, gray, red, yellow, or green

TRANSPARENCY Transparent to translucent

LUSTER Glassy to pearly

Scapolite

Previously known as wernerite and dipyre, this silicate is known for its large crystals. The largest ones usually grow in marble.

HARDNESS 5–6   **SG** 2.5– 2.7

COLOR Colorless, white, gray, yellow, orange, or pink

TRANSPARENCY Transparent to opaque

LUSTER Glassy

Diopside

Diopside is found in metamorphic rocks that were once limestones or dolomites, and in some igneous rocks such as kimberlite. The mineral occurs in the rocks of the Tyrol mountains in Austria and Italy, and in the United States.

HARDNESS	6
SG	3.3
COLOR	White, pale to dark green, violet-blue
TRANSPARENCY	Transparent to translucent
LUSTER	Glassy

Rhodonite

This silicate was named for its color from the Greek word *rhodon*, meaning "rose." Rhodonite is widely used in making beads and jewelry, even though it is fragile and has to be carefully polished.

HARDNESS	6	**SG**	3.5–3.7
COLOR	Pink to rose-red		
TRANSPARENCY	Translucent		
LUSTER	Glassy		

Jadeite

Jadeite is one of the two minerals that are commonly called jade. The other variety is nephrite. For the ancient Indians, jadeite was a symbol of life, and regarded as precious as gold. Myanmar is a major source of the mineral and ancient jadeite tools have been found there.

HARDNESS	6–7	**SG**	3.2–3.4
COLOR	White, green, lilac, pink, brown, orange, yellow, red, blue, or black		
TRANSPARENCY	Transparent to translucent		
LUSTER	Glassy to greasy		

Augite

This mineral is commonly found in dark-colored igneous rocks. It also occurs in some metamorphic rocks and meteorites, and can even be found on the Moon.

HARDNESS	5.5–6	**SG**	3.3
COLOR	Greenish-black to black, dark green, brown		
TRANSPARENCY	Translucent to nearly opaque		
LUSTER	Glassy to dull		

Richterite

Richterite is a rare manganese stone usually found in igneous rocks and limestones. It was named after the German mineralogist Theodore Richter in 1865. It is mainly used for decorative purposes.

HARDNESS	5–6
SG	3–3.5
COLOR	Brown, yellow, red, or green
TRANSPARENCY	Transparent to translucent
LUSTER	Glassy

Hornblende

Recent studies have discovered that hornblende is a group of minerals and not a single form of a mineral. However, only detailed analysis can tell them all apart. Hornblende may occur with ruby in the Harts Range mountains in Australia.

HARDNESS	5–6
SG	3.1–3.3
COLOR	Green, black
TRANSPARENCY	Translucent to opaque
LUSTER	Glassy

Nephrite

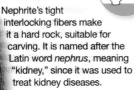

Nephrite's tight interlocking fibers make it a hard rock, suitable for carving. It is named after the Latin word *nephrus*, meaning "kidney," since it was used to treat kidney diseases.

HARDNESS	6.5
SG	2.9–3.4
COLOR	Cream, light to dark green
TRANSPARENCY	Translucent to nearly opaque
LUSTER	Dull to waxy

Riebeckite

This mineral was once valued for its fireproofing qualities and its ability to withstand electricity and acid, but scientists later discovered that the fibers are harmful to people and caused diseases.

HARDNESS	6
SG	3.3–3.4
COLOR	Dark blue, black
TRANSPARENCY	Transparent to translucent
LUSTER	Glassy, silky

Emerald

The green variety of the mineral beryl is known as emerald. To the Egyptians, it was a symbol of fertility and life. The finest emeralds, such as those in the British Crown Jewels, come from Colombia, where they have been mined for centuries.

HARDNESS 7.5–8

SG 2.6–3

COLOR Green

TRANSPARENCY Transparent to translucent

LUSTER Glassy

Cordierite

This mineral was named after French geologist Pierre L. A. Cordier. Gem-quality cordierite is also called "water sapphire" after its blue color.

HARDNESS 7–7.5 **SG** 2.6

COLOR Blue, blue-green, gray-violet

TRANSPARENCY Transparent to translucent

LUSTER Glassy to greasy

Vesuvianite

The crystals of vesuvianite are cut and polished for collectors but the transparent variety is too soft to wear. It forms when limestone undergoes changes due to heat and pressure.

HARDNESS 6.5

SG 3.4

COLOR Green, yellow

TRANSPARENCY Transparent to translucent

LUSTER Glassy to resinous

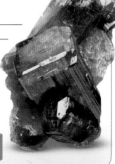

Hemimorphite

Rounded masses, usually colorless

Hemimorphite gets its name from the Greek *hemi*, meaning "half," and *morphe,* meaning "form," which is a reference to its unique crystal form. The two ends of each crystal are of different shapes, which is rare in minerals.

HARDNESS 4.5–5	SG 3.4–3.5
COLOR Colorless, white, yellow, blue, or green	
TRANSPARENCY Transparent to translucent	
LUSTER Glassy	

Talc

One of the Earth's softest minerals, talc is ground finely to make talcum powder. It is the main ingredient of soapstone and has been traditionally carved to make ornaments. Talc is also used in paints and for making paper.

HARDNESS 1	SG 2.8

COLOR White, colorless, green, yellow to brown

TRANSPARENCY Translucent

LUSTER Pearly to greasy

Muscovite

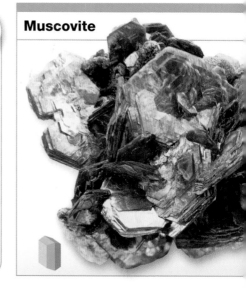

Pyrophyllite

The name of this mineral is based on the Greek words for "fire" and "leaf" because it sheds thin, leaflike layers when heated. It provides a sheen to lipsticks and is also used as a filler in paints and rubber and in dusting powders. The ancient Chinese carved it into small images and ornaments.

HARDNESS 1–2	SG 2.7–2.9

COLOR White, colorless, brown-green, pale blue, gray

TRANSPARENCY Transparent to translucent

LUSTER Pearly to dull

Muscovite forms flat sheets and, though it looks brittle, is a tough mineral. It is also called isinglass—a reference to its use in window panes in Russia. It is a member of the mica group of minerals.

HARDNESS	2.5
SG	2.8

COLOR Colorless, silver-white, pale green, rose, brown

TRANSPARENCY Transparent to translucent

LUSTER Glassy

Biotite

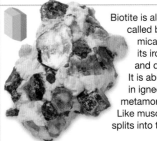

Biotite is also called black mica because of its iron content and dark color. It is abundant in igneous and metamorphic rocks. Like muscovite, it splits into thin sheets.

HARDNESS 2.5–3	**SG** 2.7–3.4

COLOR Black, brown, pale yellow, tan, or bronze

TRANSPARENCY Transparent to translucent

LUSTER Glassy to submetallic

Serpentine

There are 16 varieties of serpentine, which is named for its snakeskinlike texture. Serpentine was carved into vases and bowls on the island of Crete by the Minoans around 3,000–1,100 BCE.

HARDNESS	3.5–5.5
SG	2.5–2.6

COLOR White, gray, yellow, green, or greenish-blue

TRANSPARENCY Translucent to opaque

LUSTER Glassy to greasy, resinous, earthy, dull

Chrysocolla

Fine texture

The Greek philosopher Theophrastus used the term "chrysocolla" to refer to various materials used to bind together pieces of gold. *Chrysos* is "gold" and *kola* is "glue" in Greek. The mineral is found worldwide.

HARDNESS 2–4	**SG** 2–2.4
COLOR Blue, blue-green	
TRANSPARENCY Translucent to nearly opaque	
LUSTER Glassy to earthy	

Apophyllite

Once thought to be a single mineral, apophyllite is now known to have two varieties. Both separate into layers when heated. Colorless and green specimens from India are sometimes cut and polished as collector's gems. Crystals up to 8 in (20 cm) long are found in Bento Gonsalves, Brazil.

Blocklike crystals

HARDNESS 4.5–5

SG 2.3–2.4

COLOR Colorless pink, green, or yellow

TRANSPARENCY Transparent to translucent

LUSTER Glassy

Prehnite

Named after its discoverer Hendrik von Prehn, a Dutch military officer, prehnite is often found lining cavities in volcanic rocks. It is commonly found with the mineral zeolite and the two may be confused with one another. Transparent prehnite from Australia and Scotland is a collector's item. It is also sold under the name Cape emerald.

HARDNESS 6–6.5	**SG** 2.9

COLOR Green, yellow, tan, or white

TRANSPARENCY Transparent to translucent

LUSTER Glassy

Organic gems

Organic gems form when living things or the substances they give off fossilize over a long period of time. They are softer than rock gems and so have been used as decorative items since ancient times.

FOCUS ON...
PEARLS
Different types of pearl form depending on the shellfish and its environment.

Amber

Amber is the fossilized resin or sap of conifer trees. Sometimes it contains trapped insects. Mostly transparent, some pieces of amber are cloudy due to the air trapped inside. Its softness allows it to be carved into jewelry.

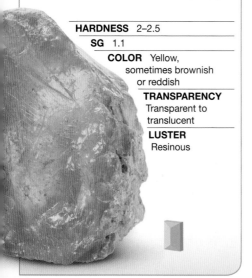

HARDNESS	2–2.5
SG	1.1
COLOR	Yellow, sometimes brownish or reddish
TRANSPARENCY	Transparent to translucent
LUSTER	Resinous

Coral

Coral comes from the skeletons of tiny sea animals. It can be polished to bring out its beautiful colors, and is easily carved into figures or beads. The most valuable coral is red.

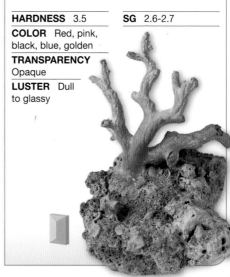

HARDNESS	3.5	**SG**	2.6-2.7
COLOR	Red, pink, black, blue, golden		
TRANSPARENCY	Opaque		
LUSTER	Dull to glassy		

▲ Freshwater pearls come from mussels. They are attached to the shell and so are flat on one side when removed.

▲ Marine-cultured pearls are grown in the sea using oyster shells and often have uniform shapes and sizes.

▲ Mother of pearl is a hard layer that lines the insides of some shellfish. It has been used for making utensils for a long time.

Shell

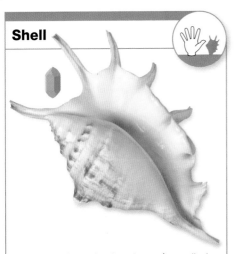

This is a hard covering found on many mollusks. Shells are made of calcite, which shellfish take in from seawater. They are used in inlays, beads, and in other decorative items.

HARDNESS 2.5	**SG** About 1.3
COLOR Red, pink, brown, blue, golden	
TRANSPARENCY Translucent to opaque	
LUSTER Dull to glassy	

Pearl

Pearl forms in certain shellfish, especially oysters. Gem-quality pearls come from oysters of tropical seas. The best and the most valuable pearls are perfectly round, but many are egg- or pear-shaped.

HARDNESS 3	**SG** 2.7
COLOR White, cream, black, blue, yellow, green, or pink	
TRANSPARENCY Opaque	
LUSTER Pearly	

Blister pearls

Dominican amber is around 25 million years old

AMBER
Resin from trees often traps insects and plant remains, which may become fossilized over time as the resin hardens into amber. Fossil remains found in Dominican amber can help us to understand the ecosystem of the tropical forests that existed long ago.

The periodic table

Minerals and rocks are made up of elements—pure, naturally occurring substances that cannot be broken down further. Each element is made up of atoms. The atoms in different elements contain different amounts of particles called protons, neutrons, and electrons, which affects their chemistry. Elements are arranged in a system called the periodic table according to their chemical and physical properties.

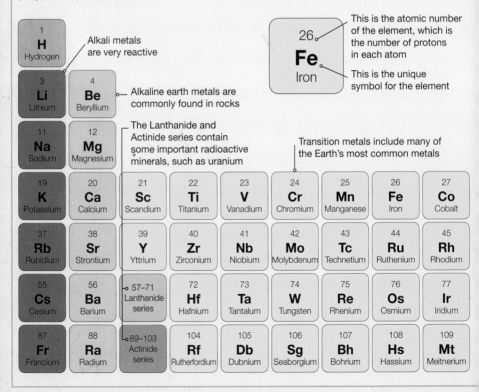

This is the atomic number of the element, which is the number of protons in each atom

26 **Fe** Iron

This is the unique symbol for the element

Alkali metals are very reactive

Alkaline earth metals are commonly found in rocks

The Lanthanide and Actinide series contain some important radioactive minerals, such as uranium

Transition metals include many of the Earth's most common metals

1 **H** Hydrogen								
3 **Li** Lithium	4 **Be** Beryllium							
11 **Na** Sodium	12 **Mg** Magnesium							
19 **K** Potassium	20 **Ca** Calcium	21 **Sc** Scandium	22 **Ti** Titanium	23 **V** Vanadium	24 **Cr** Chromium	25 **Mn** Manganese	26 **Fe** Iron	27 **Co** Cobalt
37 **Rb** Rubidium	38 **Sr** Strontium	39 **Y** Yttrium	40 **Zr** Zirconium	41 **Nb** Niobium	42 **Mo** Molybdenum	43 **Tc** Technetium	44 **Ru** Ruthenium	45 **Rh** Rhodium
55 **Cs** Cesium	56 **Ba** Barium	57–71 Lanthanide series	72 **Hf** Hafnium	73 **Ta** Tantalum	74 **W** Tungsten	75 **Re** Rhenium	76 **Os** Osmium	77 **Ir** Iridium
87 **Fr** Francium	88 **Ra** Radium	89–103 Actinide series	104 **Rf** Rutherfordium	105 **Db** Dubnium	106 **Sg** Seaborgium	107 **Bh** Bohrium	108 **Hs** Hassium	109 **Mt** Meitnerium

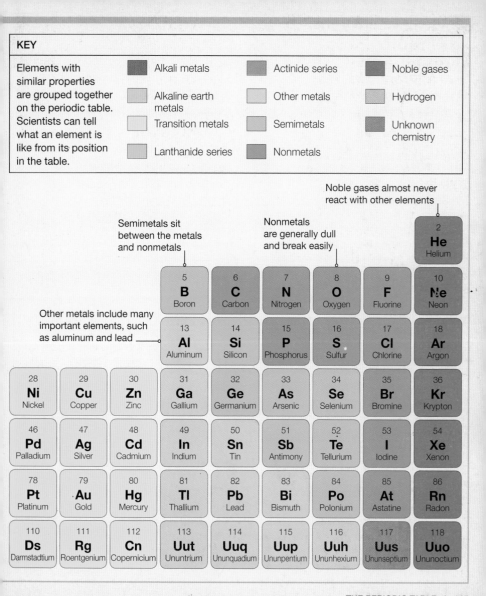

KEY

Elements with similar properties are grouped together on the periodic table. Scientists can tell what an element is like from its position in the table.

- Alkali metals
- Alkaline earth metals
- Transition metals
- Lanthanide series
- Actinide series
- Other metals
- Semimetals
- Nonmetals
- Noble gases
- Hydrogen
- Unknown chemistry

Noble gases almost never react with other elements

Semimetals sit between the metals and nonmetals

Nonmetals are generally dull and break easily

Other metals include many important elements, such as aluminum and lead

2 **He** Helium

5 **B** Boron	6 **C** Carbon	7 **N** Nitrogen	8 **O** Oxygen	9 **F** Fluorine	10 **Ne** Neon
13 **Al** Aluminum	14 **Si** Silicon	15 **P** Phosphorus	16 **S** Sulfur	17 **Cl** Chlorine	18 **Ar** Argon

28 **Ni** Nickel	29 **Cu** Copper	30 **Zn** Zinc	31 **Ga** Gallium	32 **Ge** Germanium	33 **As** Arsenic	34 **Se** Selenium	35 **Br** Bromine	36 **Kr** Krypton
46 **Pd** Palladium	47 **Ag** Silver	48 **Cd** Cadmium	49 **In** Indium	50 **Sn** Tin	51 **Sb** Antimony	52 **Te** Tellurium	53 **I** Iodine	54 **Xe** Xenon
78 **Pt** Platinum	79 **Au** Gold	80 **Hg** Mercury	81 **Tl** Thallium	82 **Pb** Lead	83 **Bi** Bismuth	84 **Po** Polonium	85 **At** Astatine	86 **Rn** Radon
110 **Ds** Darmstadtium	111 **Rg** Roentgenium	112 **Cn** Copernicium	113 **Uut** Ununtrium	114 **Uuq** Ununquadium	115 **Uup** Ununpentium	116 **Uuh** Ununhexium	117 **Uus** Ununseptium	118 **Uuo** Ununoctium

Rock facts

LANDMARK ROCK FORMATIONS

▶ The **Rock of Gibraltar** is a huge mass of limestone at the southern tip of Spain. It rises 1,400 ft (426 m) above the sea.

▶ **Shiprock Pinnacle** in New Mexico is the remains of a 27-million-year-old volcanic vent that stands 1,640 ft (500 m) above the surrounding plain. It is considered sacred by the Navajo people.

▶ **Giant's Causeway** in Northern Ireland is a collection of 40,000 basalt pillars formed 50–60 million years ago. The tallest pillars can measure up to 82 ft (25 m) high.

▶ **Ayer's Rock**, or **Uluru**, in Australia is a giant outcrop of ancient sandstone that stands 1,142 ft (348 m) high and measures 5.8 miles (9.4 km) around its base.

▶ **Delicate Arch**, in Utah, formed from weathered sandstone that has naturally eroded into a graceful arch that is 45 ft (13.5 m) high and wide enough to drive trucks through.

METEORITES

Around 20,000 meteorites fall from space to the Earth every year. Most are small, but some larger ones weigh many tons.

• **Willamette meteorite** landed in Oregon in 1906. It weighed more than 15.6 tons (14.2 metric tons)—more than the weight of three elephants.

• **Zagami meteorite** landed in Nigeria in 1962. It weighed 40 lb (18 kg) and is the largest meteorite from Mars ever found on the Earth. It started as a chunk of volcanic rock on Mars that was flung into space about 2.5 million years ago when an asteroid or comet hit Mars.

• **Y000593 meteorite** landed in Antarctica in 2000. It weighed 30.2 lb (13.7 kg), about the same as 240 eggs.

• **Sayh al Uhaymir 008** landed in Oman in 1999. It weighed almost 19 lb (8.5 kg)—as much as a small dog.

• **Nakhla meteorite** landed in El-Nakhla village, Egypt, in 1911. It weighed 11 lb (5 kg)—as much as five bags of sugar.

A typical meteorite enters the Earth's atmosphere at 6–44 miles (10–70 km) per second.

ROCK ELEMENTS

More than 98 percent of all rocks in the world are formed from a combination of just eight elements.

Element	% of all rocks
Oxygen	46.5
Silicon	27.6
Aluminum	8
Iron	5
Calcium	3 .6
Sodium	2.8
Potassium	2.6
Magnesium	2
Total	**98.1%**

BUILDING WITH ROCK

A large building, such as a bank or town hall, can be like a rock museum—it's a chance to see how useful rocks are in everyday life.

★ **Granite** can be used for the base of walls because it is very tough.

★ .The columns and steps of entrances are often made with white **limestone**.

★ Important buildings often have floors of **marble** because it looks beautiful when polished.

CLAY

Clay is a versatile sedimentary rock that is used for much more than just pots.

♦ Clay is used to make ceramic tiles, pottery, porcelain, bathtubs, sinks, drainpipes, bricks, and also firebricks for chimneys and furnaces.

♦ It is used in textiles to give weight to the fabric, and in papermaking to give paper a gloss.

♦ Wild macaws often peck on clay at riverbanks. It helps them to digest the poisons in some of the seeds they eat.

♦ Elephants lick clay from mud holes. This helps them to digest leaves they have eaten during the day.

♦ Kaolinite is a type of clay used in many indigestion remedies for people.

♦ Clay helps soil to retain the fertilizer chemicals it obtains from manure, and also helps plants to grow by absorbing ammonia and other gases. However, too much clay will make the soil heavy, preventing water and air from seeping in.

♦ Fuller's earth is a clay material used to purify fats.

Most rocks are hard and stiff, but a few are flexible. A rare type of sandstone found in India can be bent in your hands.

Mineral facts

MOST VALUABLE DIAMONDS

Koh-i-Noor is the largest and purest diamond in the world. It weighs 109 carats (0.77 oz/21.8 g) and is considered priceless.

The **Sancy diamond** was once owned by the Great Mughals of India. This priceless diamond weighs 55.23 carats (0.39 oz/11.05 g).

The **Cullinan** diamond is valued at $400 million. It was found in 1905 and weighed 3,106.75 carats (21.9 oz/621.35 g) before being cut into 9 large and 96 smaller stones.

The **Hope diamond** weighs 45.52 carats (0.32 oz/9.1 g) and is worth $350 million—but is said to bring bad luck.

MINING FOR MINERALS

• The earliest mines were small pits and tunnels that were dug about 8,000 years ago. They were mines for flint, a rock used to make tools, spears, and arrowheads.

• The first mines for metal were dug about 5,500 years ago. Tin and copper ores were crushed and heated together to make bronze.

• The deepest mines are the gold mines of South Africa. The record holder is Western Deep Levels Mine. Some of its tunnels are 2.2 miles (3.5 km) below the surface.

• Not all mines are holes in the ground. Along the coast of Namibia, Africa, large ships vacuum up sand from the ocean floor and sift it for diamonds.

HEALING MINERALS

People have believed for thousands of years that the crystals of certain minerals can help heal the body and calm the mind, and bring good luck.

Rose quartz brings unconditional love.

Lapis lazuli promotes friendship.

Jade brings relaxation.

Bloodstone increases creativity and intuition.

Onyx changes bad habits.

Hematite relieves the stress of air travel.

Amethyst cures acne.

USEFUL MINERALS

Minerals make up 99 percent of the Earth's crust. Many are valuable and are used to make items that we need every day.

★ Aluminum is the most abundant metal found in minerals, including **bauxite** and **gibbite**. It is used to make cans and in the construction of buildings.

★ Antimony comes from the mineral **stibnite**. It is used to harden lead in batteries and cables, and to make fireworks and glass.

★ **Chromite** is a source of the metal chromium, which is used to harden steel and make machine tools, ball bearings, and kitchen utensils.

★ Copper is used in electric wires and cables, in plumbing and in kitchen utensils. It is also used to make alloys such as brass (a mixture of copper and zinc) and bronze (copper and tin). **Chalcopyrite** is the main source of copper.

★ **Feldspar** is the one of the Earth's most common minerals. It is used in making glass and ceramics, and in soaps, abrasives, cement, and concrete.

★ **Fluorspar** is used to make acid for the production of nonstick coatings on pans. It is also used in toothpaste.

★ Iron is a metal found in minerals such as **hematite**. It is used to make steel, magnets, and car parts.

★ Lead is a metal found in the mineral **galena** and is used to make batteries and television tubes.

There are more than 4,500 known minerals in the world. Only 100 are common—the rest are rarer than gold.

★ Limestone is a rock made mostly of the mineral **calcite**. It is used in the construction of buildings and in making cement, paper, plastic, and glass.

★ Manganese is used in making steel, and in dyes, alloys, and batteries. It is obtained from ore minerals including **pyrolusite**.

★ **Mica** is a group of important minerals that are used in paints, plastics, and rubber.

★ **Nickel** is a native element that is used to make stainless steel.

★ The native element **silver** is used to make jewelry, cutlery, and coins.

GLOSSARY

Acid A chemical that contains a reactive form of the hydrogen atom. This readily attacks other chemicals.

Atom The basic unit of an element.

Adamantine luster A particularly brilliant shine as shown by diamond.

Asteroid A chunk of rock smaller than a planet that orbits the Sun.

Atmosphere The blanket of gases surrounding the Earth or another planet.

Bed A thin layer of sedimentary rock.

Breccia A sedimentary rock made up of angular fragments.

Canyon A deep, steep-sided valley, typically cut by a river.

Carat The standard measure of weight for precious stones and metals. A carat is equal to 0.007 oz (0.2 g).

Chondrite A stony meteorite containing tiny granules of pyroxene and olivine.

Cleavage The way a mineral or rock breaks along a certain plane, or in a certain direction.

Concretions Usually rounded, rock masses formed and found in beds of shale or clay.

Core The Earth's hot, dense iron-rich center—liquid on the outside and solid on the inside.

Crystal A naturally occurring substance whose atoms are arranged in a regular manner.

Crystal system The systems into which crystals are grouped based on their symmetry. There are six crystal systems: cubic, monoclinic, triclinic, trigonal/hexagonal, orthorhombic, and tetragonal.

Crust The Earth's rigid, outermost layer. It is divided into thicker, older continental crust (mainly granite) and thinner, more recent oceanic crust (mainly basalt).

Detrital A type of sediment that has settled in water or has been deposited by water.

Dull luster A shine that reflects very little.

Dyke A thin, sheetlike igneous intrusion that cuts across older rock structures.

Dynamic pressure The process by which an existing rock changes due to pressure alone to form metamorphic rocks.

Earthy luster A nonreflective mineral luster.

Element A substance that cannot be broken down further.

Erosion A slow process in which rocks are worn away by moving water, ice, and wind.

Eruption A discharge of lava, ash, or gas from a volcanic cone or vent.

Evaporite A natural salt or mineral left behind after the water it was dissolved in has dried up.

Extrusive rock A rock that forms when lava flows onto the Earth's surface, cools, and solidifies.

Faces The external flat surfaces that make up a crystal's shape.

Fault An extended fracture in rock along which rock masses move.

Fluorescence The optical effect whereby a mineral appears a different color in ultraviolet light than in ordinary daylight.

Foliation A pattern formed when different minerals separate within a metamorphic rock.

Fold Bends in rock strata (layers) caused by the movement of tectonic plates.

Fossil Any record of past life preserved in rocks, including bones, shells, footprints, and dung.

Fracture The distinctive way in which a mineral breaks.

Gemstone A mineral, usually crystal-like, which is valued for its color, rarity, and hardness.

Geologist A scientist who studies the Earth and its structure and composition.

Groundmass Compact, fine-grained mineral material in which larger crystals are embedded.

Habit The general shape of a mineral.

Hydrothermal vein A crack in rock through which hot mineral waters circulate due to volcanic activity. As the waters cool, minerals start to crystallize, forming gemstones and ores.

Intrusive rock A rock that forms when magma solidifies below the Earth's crust.

Igneous rock A rock formed from solidification of lava or magma on or below the Earth's surface.

Iridescence A play of colors that looks like oil on water that occurs when light reflects off internal elements of a rock or mineral.

Lava Magma that has flowed onto the Earth's surface through a volcanic opening.

Luster The way in which light reflects off the surface of a mineral.

Magma Molten rock found deep inside the Earth.

Mantle The middle layer of the Earth, between the core and the crust. It consists of hot, dense rocks, such as peridotite.

Metallic luster A shine like that of polished metal.

Metamorphic rock A rock formed when other rocks are transformed by heat, or pressure, or both.

Meteor A meteoroid (rock and dust debris in space) that enters the Earth's atmosphere and appears as a shooting star.

Meteorite A meteoroid that reaches the surface of the Earth.

Mineral A naturally occurring solid with specific characteristics, such as a particular chemical composition and crystal shape.

Mineralogist A scientist who studies minerals.

Native element A chemical element found in nature in its pure form.

Nodule A hard, rounded, stony lump found in sedimentary rock, typically made from calcite, silica, pyrite, or gypsum.

Oolitic A rock that forms from ooliths, which are individual round grains of sediment. Most ooliths are made of calcite.

Opaque A substance or material that does not let light pass through it.

Ore A rock or mineral from which a metal can be extracted.

Organic Relating to living things.

Prism A solid geometric figure with a set of faces parallel to one another.

Pluton Any body of intrusive igneous rock.

Quarry A place where stone is dug up.

Regional change The process by which an existing rock changes due to heat and pressure to form metamorphic rocks.

Resinous luster A shine like that of resin.

Rock A solid mixture of minerals. There are three types: igneous, metamorphic, and sedimentary.

Secondary mineral A mineral that replaces another as a result of weathering or other alteration process.

Sediments Particles of rock, mineral, or organic matter that are carried by wind, water, and ice.

Sedimentary rock A rock formed from sediments that have been cemented together by weathering or burial.

Semimetal A chemical element that shares some properties with metals and some with nonmetals.

Sill A thin, sheetlike, igneous intrusion that forms between layers of existing rocks.

Specific gravity The ratio of a mineral's weight compared to the weight of an equal volume of water.

Streak The color of a mineral's powder. It is less variable than the color of mineral, so is a more reliable identification tool.

Tectonic plate One of about 12 huge, floating rock slabs that make up the rigid outer layer of the Earth's crust.

Thermal contact The process by which an existing rock changes due to heat alone to form metamorphic rock.

Uplift The result of rock structures being raised upward by the movement of tectonic plates. Sediments formed on the sea bed may be uplifted to become mountains.

Vitreous luster A shine like that of glass.

Volcano The site of an eruption of lava and hot gases from within the Earth. Magma flows up a central passage and erupts as lava.

Weathering The slow breakdown of rock by long exposure to the weather, including moisture, frost, and rainwater.

Index

A

acanthite 77
Acasta gneiss 5
achondrite 52
actinolite 63
adamite 113
agate 124
alabaster 119
aluminum 149
amber 61, 67, 140, 142–3
amethyst 123, 148
amphibolite 44–5
andalusite 129
andesite 23
ankerite 107
anorthosite 26
anthracite 32
antimony 76, 149
apatite 64, 112
apophyllite 138–9
aquamarine 66, 67
aragonite 106
arkose 37
arsenates 60, 110–13
arsenic 72, 80, 86
arsenopyrite 86–7
art materials 30
artinite 109
asteroids 52
atacamite 101
atennantite 90
atmosphere 5
atoms 6, 144
augite 132

aurichalcite 107
Ayer's Rock (Uluru) 146
azurite 109

B

banded gneiss 9, 50–1
baryte 121
barytocalcite 108
basalt 18, 20
bauxite 59, 98, 149
beryl 63
biotite 137
bismuth 72
bismuthinite 84
bloodstone 124, 148
borates 60, 116–17
borax 116
bornite 77
boron 116
boulangerite 90
bournonite 90, 91
breccia 36–7
brochantite 121
brookite 96–7

C

calcite 56, 64, 104–5, 149
cancrinite 127
carbonates 60, 104–9
carnallite 101
carnotite 112
cassiterite 94

chalcanthite 61, 120–1
chalcocite 81, 88
chalcophyllite 112
chalcopyrite 65, 81, 149
chalk 30, 31, 104
chert 34
chromates 61, 118–21
chromite 93, 95, 149
chrysoberyl 95
chrysocolla 6, 138
cinnabar 58, 65, 76, 78–9
citrine 123
clay 30, 38, 147
cleavage 62
cobaltite 85
collecting 10–13
color 64
concretions 39
conglomerate 37
copper 63, 68, 76, 88–9, 148, 149
coral 61, 67, 104, 140
cordierite 134
core, Earth's 4
corundum 64, 92, 93
covellite 78
craters, meteorite 52–3
crocoite 65, 118
crust, Earth's 5, 17
cryolite 100, 101
crystals 6, 62, 148
cuprite 93
cutting 66

D

dacite 26
Danakil Desert 74–5
Delicate Arch 146
Devil's Tower 21, 28–9
diamond 6, 7, 22, 58, 64, 67, 71, 148
diaspore 98
diopside 132
diorite 22
dolerite 21
dolomite 15, 31, 108
dyke 16

E

Earth 4–5
eclogite 49
elements 6, 144–5, 147
emerald 7, 67, 134
erosion 16, 17
erythrite 60, 113
evaporites 56

F

feldspar 7, 8, 61, 149
feldspathic gritstone 35
ferberite 120
flint 35, 148
fluorite 64, 100, 101
fluorspar 149
folded schist 19
foliation 18
fossils 15, 19, 140, 143
fracture 62
freshwater limestone 19
fulgurite 45

G

gabbro 8–9
galena 65, 76, 149
garnet 61
gemstones 66–7, 122
geologists 8
Giant's Causeway 21, 146
gibbite 149
gneiss 5, 9, 48–9, 50–1
goethite 99
gold 58, 68, 69, 148
grains 18–19
granite 18, 21, 147
graphite 6, 71
green chrysocolla 6
greenockite 79
grossular 128–9
gypsum 31, 64, 119, 120

H

habit 62
halides 59, 100–1
halite 100, 102–3
hardness 64
hauerite 85
healing minerals 148
heat 16, 17, 19, 57
hematite 41, 65, 95, 148, 149
hemimorphite 135
hornblende 133
hornfels 44
howlite 117

hydrocarbons 7
hydroxides 59, 98–9

I

Iceland spar 62
igneous minerals 57
igneous rocks 5, 8, 9, 16, 18, 20–9
ignimbrite 24
iron 4, 7, 71, 76, 149
ironstone 38

J

jade 122, 132, 148
jadeite 132
jamesonite 90
jasper 64
jet 67

KL

kimberlite 22
Koh-i-Noor 67, 148
kyanite 128–9
lapis lazuli 148
lava 5, 16, 18, 57
lazurite 126
lead 76, 149
leucite 126
limestone 19, 30, 147, 149
limonite 99
loess 34
luster 65

M

magma 4, 15, 16, 17, 18, 20, 57
magnesite 108
magnetite 7, 94
malachite 55, 60, 106
manganese 149
mantle, Earth's 4
marble 19, 42, 43, 104, 105
marcasite 84–5
megagems 67
mercury 73, 76
metamorphic minerals 57
metamorphic rocks 8, 9, 16, 17, 19, 42–9
meteorites 52–3, 146
mica 61
micaceous sandstone 38
migmatite 47
millerite 83
millet-seed sandstone 19
mimetite 113
mineralogists 7
minerals 54–143
  composition of 6
  facts 148–9
  formation of 56–7
  groups 7, 58–61
  identifying 62–5
  useful 149
mining 7, 148
Mohs' scale 64
molybdates 61, 118–21
molybdenite 65, 87
muscovite 136–7
mylonite 48

N

Nakhla meteorite 146
native elements 58, 68–75, 149
natrolite 61, 131
nephrite 133
nickel 149
nickel-iron 72
nitrates 60, 116–17
nitratine 117
nodules 39

O

obsidian 9, 20, 62
oil 7
olivine 8, 9, 57, 130–1
onyx 124–5, 148
opal 67, 122, 125
ore minerals 7, 59, 98
ores 92–3
organic gems 67, 140–3
organic minerals 61
orpiment 65, 84
orthoclase 127
oxides 59, 92–7

P

pearl 61, 67, 140–1
peat 32
pegmatite 27
Pélé's hair 24–5
pentlandite 78
peridot 130, 131
peridotite 18, 23
periodic table 144–5
perovskite 95

phonolite 22, 29
phosgenite 108
phosphates 60, 110–13
phyllite 42
pink granite 18
plagioclase feldspar 8
platinum 69, 76
pluton 16
polishing 66
polybasite 90
porphyry 27
precious gems 67
prehnite 139
pressure 16, 17, 19, 42, 57
proustite 58, 90, 91
pumice 24
pyrargyrite 91
pyrite 58, 84–5
pyrochlore 97
pyrolusite 149
pyromorphite 110
pyrophyllite 136
pyroxene 8, 9
pyrrhotite 79

QR

quartz 58, 61, 64, 65, 122, 123
quartzite 44–5
realgar 80
record keeping 11
red sandstone 9
regional change 17
rhodochrosite 106–7
rhodonite 132
rhomb porphyry 27
rhyolite 22–3
richterite 133

riebeckite 133
rock crystal 122
rock cycle 16
Rock of Gibraltar 146
rock gypsum 31
rock salt 31
rock-forming minerals 7
rocks 14–53
  age of 5
  composition of 8–9
  facts 146–7
  formation of 16–17
  identifying 18–19
  types of 9
rose quartz 123, 148
ruby 7, 66, 67, 92
rutile 59, 97

S

Salar de Uyuni 102–3
salt 100, 102–3
samarskite 96
sandstone 9, 19, 36, 38,
  40–1, 147
sapphire 67, 93
sard 125
Sayh al Uhaymir 008
  meteorite 146
scapolite 131
scheelite 121
schist 19, 43
scolecite 63
sedimentary minerals 56
sedimentary rocks 8, 9, 16,
  17, 19, 30–41
semiprecious gems 67
septarian nodule 39
serpentine 137

serpentinite 47
shale 36
shell 141
Shiprock Pinnacle 146
siderite 105
silicates 4, 18, 61, 122–39
sill 16
sillimanite 129
silver 69, 76, 149
skarn 46
slate 43
smithsonite 104
specific gravity 64
specimens
  cleaning 12
  labeling 12
  storage and display 13
sphalerite 77
spinel 57, 94
stannite 81
stibnite 76, 82, 149
stony-iron meteorites 53
strata 17
streak 65
strontianite 109
sulfates 61, 118–21
sulfides 58, 76–89
sulfosalts 58, 90–1
sulfur 70, 74–5, 76, 90
syenite 26
sylvanite 87
sylvite 59

T

talc 64, 136
tectonic plates 5
tektite 52
tetrahedrite 90

tin 148
titanium 93
tools, collecting 11
topaz 64, 67, 122, 128
trachyte 27
transparency 65
travertine 33
trona 109
tufa 34–5
tuff 15, 25
tungstates 61, 118–21
turquoise 111, 114–15

UV

uranite 96
vanadates 60, 110–13
variscite 110
veins, mineral 56
vesuvianite 134
volcanic activity 5, 16

W

The Wave 40–1
wavellite 111
weathering 16, 17, 29
Willamette meteorite 146
wulfenite 56, 119

YZ

Y000593 meteorite 146
Zagami meteorite 146
zinc 76
zincite 94
zinkenite 90
zircon 66, 128

Acknowledgments

Dorling Kindersley would like to thank: Monica Byles for proofreading; Helen Peters for indexing; David Roberts and Rob Campbell for database creation; Claire Bowers, Fabian Harry, Romaine Werblow, and Rose Horridge for DK Picture Library assistance; Ritu Mishra, Nasreen Habib, and Neha Chaudhary for editorial assistance; and Isha Nagar for design assistance.

The publishers would also like to thank the following for their kind permission to reproduce their photographs:

(Key: a-above; b-below/bottom; c-center; f-far; l-left; r-right; t-top)

2–3 Corbis: Walter Geiersperger (c). 5 Getty Images: Toshi Sasaki / Stone+ (tr); Science & Society Picture Library (tc). 6 Dorling Kindersley: Natural History Museum, London (ca). Getty Images: Siede Preis / Photodisc (bl). 7 Alamy Images: E.D. Torial (b). Dorling Kindersley: Natural History Museum, London (tl, cr). Getty Images: f8 Imaging / Hulton Archive (tr). 8–9 Science Photo Library: Dirk Wiersma (c). 10 Alamy Images: Tom Grundy (cl). Dorling Kindersley: Natural History Museum, London (br). 11 Dorling Kindersley: Natural History Museum, London (tl, br). 12 Dorling Kindersley: Natural History Museum, London (tc). 12–13 Dorling Kindersley: Natural History Museum, London (c). 14 Corbis: Frans Lanting. 15 Corbis: Atlantide Phototravel. 18 Dorling Kindersley: Oxford University Museum of Natural History (cl). 19 Dorling Kindersley: Natural History Museum, London (bl). 20 Dorling Kindersley: Natural History Museum, London (cl). 21 Corbis: Granville Harris / Eye Ubiquitous (tl). Getty Images: Jeff Foott / Discovery Channel Images (tc). 24–25 Dorling Kindersley: Natural History Museum, London (b). 28–29 Dreamstime.com: Natalia Bratslavsky. 30 Dorling Kindersley: Judith Miller / Freeman's (tl); Natural History Museum, London (bl, bl/Powdered Clay). 32 Dorling Kindersley: Natural History Museum, London (tl). 40–41 Alamy Images: Pritz / F1online digitale Bildagentur GmbH. 42 Dorling Kindersley: Rough Guides (tl). 50–51 Getty Images: Andreas Strauss / LOOK. 54 Dorling Kindersley: The Smithsonian Institution, Washington DC. 55 Dorling Kindersley: Judith Miller / 333 Auctions LLC. 56 Dorling Kindersley: Natural History Museum, London (c). 56–57 Alamy Images: Photoshot Holdings Ltd (b). 57 Dorling Kindersley: Natural History Museum, London (tl). 58 Dorling Kindersley: Natural History Museum, London (tl, br). 62 Dorling Kindersley: Oxford University Museum of Natural History (br). 63 Dorling Kindersley: Natural History Museum, London (tr). 65 Dorling Kindersley: Natural History Museum, London (c, br). 66 Dorling Kindersley: Natural History Museum, London (tl). 67 Corbis: Corbis Art (tl). Dorling Kindersley: Natural History Museum, London (bc). Getty Images: Tim Graham (cr). 68 Dorling Kindersley: Natural History Museum, London (br); The Science Museum, London (cl). NASA: Human Spaceflight Collection (bl). 71 Dorling Kindersley: Oxford University Museum of Natural History (tr). 73 Dorling Kindersley: Natural History Museum, London (cl). 74–75 Getty Images: Radius Images. 76 Getty Images: Dea / A. Dagli Orti (cl); Steve Eason / Hulton Archive (tl). 77 Dorling Kindersley: Natural History Museum, London (cl). 88–89 Corbis: Peter Ginter / Science Faction. 90 Alamy Images: De Schuyter Marc / Arterra Picture Library (tl). Corbis: Macduff Everton (cl). SuperStock: imagebroker.net (bl). 92 Dorling Kindersley: Natural History Museum, London (br). 102–103 Corbis: Bertrand Gardel / Hemis. 114–115 Corbis: Randy Faris. 119 Dorling Kindersley: Dan Bannister (tl). 122 Dorling Kindersley: Judith Miller / Blanchet et Associes (tl); Judith Miller / Sylvie Spectrum (tl); Judith Miller / Lynn & Brian Holmes (bl). 124 Dorling Kindersley: The Smithsonian Institution, Washington DC (tl). 127 Dorling Kindersley: Natural History Museum, London (tr). 132 Dorling Kindersley: Natural History Museum, London (tr). 141 Dorling Kindersley: Natural History Museum, London (tr). 142–143 Corbis: Jeff Daly / Visuals Unlimited.

Jacket images: Front: Dorling Kindersley: Natural History Museum, London fcrb, fcrb/ (Copper), c; Spine: Dorling Kindersley: Natural History Museum, London t.

All other images © Dorling Kindersley

For further information see: www.dkimages.com